HELENA

PRINCESS RECLAIMED

The life and times of Queen Victoria's third daughter

by

S. Chomet

Begell House

New York

ISBN 1-56700-145-9

Contents

Prologue

An imagined assignation 01

A princess is born 07

Prince Consort's new librarian 13

Placid, plump, dowdy and ...? 30

Frogmore and Cumberland Lodge 55

'A writer of some distinction' 70

The Bergsträsser affair 81

Beautiful, talented and helpful 87

St. Martin's place 90

South Africa 100

Mrs. Williams' school 111

Nursing 120

Laudanum 127

Schomberg house mysteries 133

The final years 146

Appendix, Sources and Index 153

Prologue

Princess Helena was the third of Queen Victoria's five daughters. Carl Ruland was Prince Consort's German-born librarian and sometime tutor to the Royal children. He left Windsor after three and a half years in the employment of the Royal Family. And Helena became Princess Christian (of Schleswig Holstein Sonderburg Augustenburg) when she married Prince Christian, an impoverished continental prince, in 1866.

An imagined assignation

At 2 o'clock in the morning, with the gaslights turned off, Pall Mall was at its most mysterious in the dark as Big Ben struck on the hour a mile or so away across St James' Park. Whilst most of Victorian London was by then firmly in the arms of Morpheus, an occasional dark-coated figure could still be seen profiled against the background of an unusually clear sky, hurrying from the door of a gentleman's club in the famous thoroughfare, trying to attract the attention of one of the very few horse-drawn cabs that were still around so late at night and so early in the morning.

In the heavily humid night of the summer of 1902, the quiescent urban air bore the offensively penetrating stench of horse dung left uncleared on the streets after a busy day.

A few minutes past the hour, a carriage drew up close to the main entrance of 78 Pall Mall, the historic and supremely elegant Schomberg House that was the London home of a Royal Princess and, among other things, a musical focus of the metropolis. The house was said to have better acoustics than the Opera House in Covent Garden.

The doors of both house and cab were simultaneously flung open and a handsome, though a little heavy, middle aged woman - obviously of considerable social distinction - was rapidly escorted across the pavement by a uniformed member of her domestic staff to join a man protected by darkness and shadows in the back of the cab. Both doors were then shut and the cab moved off speedily at the crack of the driver's whip.

To the Victorian driver's eye this was an assignation of unusual significance, since anyone familiar - however peripherally - with the social scene of central London of the time would have been aware of the importance of the address at which the unidentified lady was picked up. The formally attired man inside the cab was more difficult to identify by either accent or appearance. He was obviously not an Englishman, and was therefore regarded with some suspicion by the cabman who - much to his chagrin - could not overhear the politely restrained conversation taking place below him.

At the darkened west end of Pall Mall, the driver was told to turn sharply left and then right, and finally to drive ahead towards the Palace. To his great surprise, his final instruction was to enter Buckingham Palace grounds through a side gate where a startled uniformed man on duty peered intently through the cab window, instantly recognised the female figure in the cab and waved on the driver with a deferential gesture to the two passengers.

Few members of the Palace domestic staff were readily available in the palace so late at night, and it was difficult to produce any form of acceptable refreshment. But it was done, and the couple sat in a small ground-floor sitting room, heavily decorated in the Victorian manner, with gaslights hissing gently into the Faraday flues. An attentive Silesian maid, barely able to communicate in English, hovered timidly in the background.

As fine china cups filled with tea were placed before them, they haltingly exchanged short sentences in a mixture of English and German. She was more fluent in English and he in German. Contemporary records tell us that she was 56 and he 66. Shockingly for those days, there was no-one in attendance apart from the maid.

To keep the conversation flowing, he continued to ask questions, especially about the late Queen Victoria. But, of course, he already knew the answers.

'In death she was so beautiful; such peace and joy on her dear face - a radiance from heaven' - the Princess slipped instinctively into the controlled articulation that long ago the royal children were taught to adopt in the presence of others, and repeated a phrase used before elsewhere.

'When did it happen?' - he enquired.

'Eighteen months ago, on January 22' - was the expected reply. - 'Sir James Reid, the Queen's personal doctor, was in attendance throughout. The last words on her lips were the names of my brothers and sisters. The last name in her journal was mine'.

The mannered form of the conversation could not conceal the discomfort of the tense and embarrassing encounter between two people who - whatever their connection in the past - had not seen one another for half a lifetime. This was not an occasion for irregular familiarity.

After a few long minutes it became quite clear that the meeting would not be a success and he rose slowly to his feet, clicked his heels Central-European fashion and bowed his head before her.

'I am very glad indeed to have seen you again, Herr Ruland' - she said in German, offering him her right hand which he took and carefully and gently kissed.

He then turned round rather awkwardly, nearly losing his balance, and left without saying a word. She remained sitting very uprightly, her eyes fixed on the highly polished mahogany doors after they closed silently behind him.

And then, after a few steps in the corridor, he suddenly remembered that he still had in his possession - in his left breast pocket - the very private letters which Princess Helena addressed to him over forty years earlier. He intended to return them to her in person, but now it was clear that no such thing would ever be possible.

Carl Ruland in ca. 1905

Five years after the early-morning encounter in Buckingham Palace, Carl Ruland resigned from his post as Director of the Goethe Museum in Weimar, following a disagreement about an exhibition of the works of the French sculptor Rodin, which were thought by some of his German colleagues and the local establishment to be too explicit. A year later he died, having left strict instructions to his son that all his personal papers be destroyed after his death.

Princess Helena died in London in Schomberg House in 1923. Ruland's instructions were somehow partly circumvented and some of his papers survived. Indeed, Helena's teenage letters to Ruland eventually found their way back to Windsor just after World War II and now reside in the total darkness of a file in the Royal Archives in Windsor Castle. They reveal a serious flirtation between Carl Ruland and the Royal Princess, which we now know was the reason for Ruland's somewhat abrupt departure from England.

Helena's letters are in German and are accompanied by sketches made by the Princess for the handsome and brilliant young man from Frankfurt whom she admired when he was in his middle twenties and she in her teens.

Whatever happened between them then or later, it is aptly described by Vivian Grey's words to his son[1]: '...... human nature is, I imagine, much the same this moment ..... in Pall Mall .... as it was some thousand years ago ..... on the banks of Ilyssus'.

A princess is born

Victoria, crowned at 18 the Queen of Britain and Ireland, was a very prolific lady. In the space of seventeen years of a famous marriage she produced nine children, five of them daughters. 'She became a Queen as instinctively royal as Elizabeth: a Queen aware that she embodied the dignity of England'[2]. And she began by immediately circumventing an attempt by her mother, the Duchess of Kent, and her mother's Comptroller, Sir John Conroy, to control her by making her mother Regent.

Albert, the Prince Consort, whom she married in 1840 at the age of 21, died in 1861 (probably of stomach cancer, undiagnosed by incompetent physicians). Thereafter, the Queen embarked on a consciously and conspicuously cultivated widowhood for another 40 years during which she withdrew into a black-edged world of Royal isolation.

She was physically unimpressive. Increasingly plump and only just over five feet tall, she became the dominant and privately domineering figure of nineteenth century Britain.

Her biographers - of whom there have been many - describe her as scrupulously honest, shrewd rather than clever, always decisive, and possessed of great appetite and unusually good memory.

She traded loyalty with some remarkably talented and attractive men, from the 'excellent and truly kind' Lord Melbourne - prime minister at her accession - to Benjamin Disraeli, later Lord Beaconsfield, a political and literary genius with a talent for unmitigated flattery to which she responded meekly and keenly, often beyond the limits of the strict etiquette that normally ruled the minutest details of her life and the day-to-day life of her Court.

Gladstone, who followed Disraeli as Prime Minister, was a displeasing figure to her; even when he died, she could not bring herself to write the customary flattering valediction. The best she could manage was to confine herself to saying that[3] 'he was one of the most distinguished statesmen of my reign'. This was not untypical of her: in a letter to her uncle Leopold she described[4] a previous prime minister - Lord Palmerston - as having 'many valuable qualities though many bad ones' (one of the latter was perhaps exemplified by Palmerston's letter to her in which he dared to say[5] that he was sure that '..... your Majesty will never forget that you are sovereign of Great Britain'; she retaliated in subsequent letters by calling him Pilgerstein!).

The Queen had very different words for Disraeli. Her final dedication, inscribed on the monument commemorating Disraeli in the Hughenden Church, and delivered on her behalf by the Prince of Wales on March 26, 1881, reads: '.... placed by his grateful and affectionate Sovereign and friend, Victoria R.I.'

Disraeli beguiled her with extravagant letters, the contents of which she absorbed with openly declared pleasure. There were extended periods when, as Prime Minister, he sent her daily reports. 'It was part of his nature to treat women like this, and he was a genuine romantic, even sentimentalist, in his attitude to the throne'[6]. She loved it, and even instructed her daughter Helena - who acted as amanuensis to the Queen - to send him his favourite flowers[7].

In her final years, Victoria relied heavily on another male figure - Sir James Reid, her personal physician. And before that there was John Brown her faithful manservant. In all such relationships, some more formal than others, her loyalty to people she really liked could be - and often was - deep and steadfast.

On Monday, May 25, 1846, under the headline 'Accouchement of Her Majesty', *The Times* announced 'with happiness' the delivery - at Buckingham Palace - of a princess at five minutes to 3 o'clock. The *official* Bulletin was signed by James Clark (Queen's physician), Charles Lacock (*accoucher*) and Robert Ferguson (*accoucher*). Lacock got £1,000 for his work[8] and Ferguson £800. Both the Archbishop of Canterbury and the Chief Rabbi devised and published celebratory forms of prayer[9].

The Times boasted that it published a second edition announcing the happy event a mere 15 minutes after it took place and a 'full hour before any other daily or evening paper'. Clearly, in so far as publishing scoops are concerned, not much has changed over the years in the highly competitive world of newspapers, especially in matters relating to Royalty.

What the papers did not report was that this was a complicated birth. 'She came into this world rather blue' - Prince Albert wrote[10] to his brother on May 26 - 'but she is quite well now. Victoria suffered longer and more than the other times and she will have to remain very quiet to recover....'. The fair haired, blue-eyed infant recovered quite rapidly and was soon said to be doing well.

Prince Albert, the Prince Consort, was present at the delivery together with several members of the Privy Council and Ladies of the Bedchamber, as was the custom of the day. Many others, including the Queen's mother - the Duchess of Kent - were in the adjoining rooms. The list of people calling on the Royal Family that afternoon occupied - in order of rank - most of a long column of small print in *The Times.*

The young princess - Victoria's third daughter and her fifth child - was named Helena Augusta Victoria. Since the family often spoke German at home, and the German diminutive of Helena was Helenchen, her nickname was soon shortened to Lenchen. She is invariably referred to by this name in Royal family journals and letters. It was a habit of the Royal family to assign nicknames to its offspring. Thus, the Princess Royal was called Vicky, Princess Beatrice was Baby and so on.

It took no more than three years for the princess to appear again on pages devoted to chronicling royal events and the attendant gossip. The occasion was a widely reported attempt on the life of the Queen (one of a total of seven such attempts in her lifetime).

While driving down Constitution Hill on May 19, 1849, the Queen, who had Helena with her, was fired at by an unemployed Irishman called William Hamilton. The three-year old Helena delivered her own verdict on this startling event[11]: 'Man shot, tried to shoot dear Mamma, must be punished'. This must rank as an expression of Victorian morality, unrivalled in its precocity. But it was not a complete description because Hamilton fired harmless blanks and the Queen's life was not in fact in any real danger at any time. Hamilton was nevertheless sentenced to a total of seven years' transportation.

Lenchen is sometimes described as having been more engaged by physical than intellectual challenges in her childhood. On the other hand, Lady Augusta Stanley noted[12] that Helena displayed considerable talent for drawing at the age of only three. At the age of 11, she was producing very accomplished work, some of which survives in the Royal Archives.

She was said to be interested in machinery, which found a sympathetic response in her father, Prince Albert, who was intensely interested in science and engineering. Horse riding and boating were said to have been among Lenchen's other favourite childhood occupations.

All this is often contrasted with the intellectual brilliance of her oldest sister Vicky, the contemplative character of her next oldest sister Alice and the striking appearance, artistic temperament and abilities of another sister, Princess Louise. Even the musical talents of Lenchen tended to be belittled. And, generally, her character and determination were often said to have been stronger than her abilities. None of this was fair, as we shall see.

Prince Consort's new librarian

Carl Ruland was born in Frankfurt on Main on July 15, 1834. He first studied theology and then art history, literature and linguistics at Tuebingen and at Bonn. At the age of twenty five he was appointed Librarian to Prince Albert, the Prince Consort, on the recommendation of Baron Stockmar, the Prince's highly trusted adviser. Ruland was personally interviewed by Dr. Becker, the then Royal Librarian, who made sure, among other things, that Ruland was not a Catholic and had no undesirable contacts in Germany[13].

Letters written by Dr. Becker in the course of his search for a replacement for Prince Albert's librarian show that the religion of the candidate for the post was a question of some concern to the Prince. Perhaps he recalled that when he married the young Victoria in 1840, Lord Melbourne made no mention of Albert's religion in the official announcement of the proposed marriage, but the Leader of the Opposition in the Lords, Duke of Wellington, insisted that this point be made explicit[14].

Ruland received[15] the comparatively large sum of £300 per annum, paid quarterly in equal shares by Queen Victoria from the Privy Purse and by the Prince Consort himself, as were the salaries of other members of their personal staff. Ruland was provided with his own living quarters and two servants (he had to pay one of them at the rate of £25 per annum, but he did not have to pay for any of the laundry facilities!).

Carl Ruland as Prince Consort's librarian

In addition to being Prince Consort's librarian, Ruland was his amanuensis and was expected to perform some tutoring of the Royal children as well. He must have been well thought of because he was allowed to tutor the future King of England (he reported some difficulties in getting the young Prince of Wales to translate some very advanced texts into French and German).

Ruland's name first appears in England in correspondence held in the Royal Archives in Windsor Castle from which it is clear that he began his work as librarian in the summer of 1859. He did not last very long - less than four years. By 1863 he was describing himself in print as the *former* librarian, though he continued to be involved in the preparation for the press of the catalogue of what was to become known as the *Ruland/Raphael Collection.*

This designation would probably have mispleased the Queen because she discovered in the course of the new librarian's service that Princess Helena developed a crush on the knowledgeable and attractive young German. The inevitable consequence was, of course, that Ruland was sent packing back to Germany under a heavy cloud. His departure is referred to in a letter from the Queen to her eldest daughter, the Crown Princess of Prussia[16] in which she mentions Hermann Sahl as the 'permanent successor to Mr. Rulandt' [sic]. After Prince Albert's death in 1861, Ruland became German secretary to the Queen, although he is often referred to as the Librarian.

The overt reason given for Ruland's departure, in October 1863[17], was the poor state of his mother's health and the advanced

Helena in ca. 1860

age of his father. At the same time, he is somewhat pointedly described by the Queen in her letters as 'useful and able' whereas his predecessor, Dr. Ernest Becker, is referred to as 'our dear and excellent friend'. These two phrases are perhaps pointers to some heavy Victorian dissimulation. Nevertheless, the Queen was generous enough to ask General Grey, her private secretary, to look into the question of a pension for Carl Ruland who had been in the employment of the Prince Consort and then the Queen for a total of three and half years. She could get angry, but she was not mean.

Relations were not broken off entirely and Ruland returned to Windsor briefly in 1864 and 1865, probably in connection with the Raphael collection[18].

Ruland's own impressions[19] were rather different. In a letter from Windsor Castle dated December 14, 1861, he wrote to his parents about Prince Albert's death: "His death is a disaster for the entire family, for England, for the whole of Europe. What he was as a person no-one can judge better than myself. Did he not treat me as his own son? The Queen told me so herself just recently, as I was kneeling in front of her sofa. 'He liked you as much a few others' - she told me. 'Remain my friend and do not leave me and my children!'". The letter went on: 'She had Princess Alice deliver the most loving and affectionate words to me'.

Two days later he wrote again: '.... I am entering the Queen's service, and indeed in an extremely confidential role. I cannot express how her trust during this time of need has touched me'.

He went on: 'I hope you are not disappointed that I have fulfilled the Queen's wish, and will not leave her. Had I gone, what would I have done? Teach? - that no longer takes my fancy after the responsibilities I have had here. Being a writer is also an ungratifying profession. Here, on the other hand, my life and work have a meaning if - as they all say here – I can be of help to the entire family. The gratitude for the extreme graciousness with which they have treated me from the very first moment makes it impossible for me to resist their first wish, expressed under such terrible circumstances.' And yet, two years later he was gone.

Whatever may have happened meanwhile between the 'librarian' and the teenage princess, it was described over a century later in a letter from Windsor Castle as a 'mild flirtation', but further light on this is thrown by correspondence between Princess Alice and her mother, Queen Victoria.

Nearly a decade after these events, in March 1873, Princess Alice, by then the Grand Duchess of Hesse, residing in Darmstadt, undertook a cultural expedition to Italy. She travelled *incognita*, accompanied by her lady in waiting Miss Emily Hardinge and 'Hofrat' Carl Ruland. The party went from Darmstadt via Munich and the Brenner Pass to Florence, where Alice spent three days, and then went on to Rome.

On February 19, Alice reported, before leaving Darmstadt, that Ruland traveled by permission of his new employer the Grand Duke of Weimar to join her as *cicerone*. 'Mr. Ruland is an excellent cicerone for picture and sculpture' - she wrote from Rome on April 6. Clearly, Carl Ruland had by then settled down in new employment.

On the same February 19, in a letter to her first daughter Vicky - then the Crown Princess of Prussia - Queen Victoria asked Vicky to warn Alice that Ruland (again spelled Rulandt by the Queen) should not be treated with 'familiarity'. She went on to refer darkly to 'his conduct to me about what you know before Alice married Louis' (on July 1, 1862 at Osborne). She urged that Vicky should advise against Ruland accompanying Alice on this occasion[20].

'Believe me it is a bad thing' - the Queen wrote ominously[21].

Actually, the word 'familiarity' had a particular meaning to the Queen. For example, when another daughter, Louise, was being courted by the then young Lord Lorne, the Queen found it difficult to accept the *familiarity* that necessarily developed in a closer relationship with someone who was not a member or relative of the Royal family. When Lorne referred to Louise as 'dearest Louise', it was made clear to him that etiquette dictated that the word *Princess* had to be used, and was more appropriate, at *all* times[22].

Although more than ten years had passed after Ruland's departure, and Ruland had meanwhile married the renowned actress Marie Schulze in 1872, the Queen was clearly still hostile to him. The extent to which 'a bad thing' was a euphemism for what would today be described as an 'unacceptable thing' can only be guessed at. What is certain is that the Queen's hostility was equivalent to a sentence without the remotest possibility of appeal. Perhaps she remembered the words of Baron Stockmar who defined acceptable tutors to royal children as 'persons morally good, intelligent, well-informed and experienced', but above all able to 'check undesirable tendencies of adolescence'[23].

The Queen does not come out too well from all this. Ruland was obviously a sincere young man (even if he did have an eye for a pretty princess or even two) and he served his royal master and mistress as well as he could. His final reward was the sack and a pension. It could have been worse: the sack alone.

Ruland's departure, engineered by the Queen, was not the last time a daughter's amorosity was radically excised by the Royal parent. This happened again when Helena's younger sister, Princess Louise fell in love with Prince Leopold's Instructor (later Governor), the Reverend Robin(son) Duckworth.

Duckworth was a distinguished and handsome scholar, with a 'First' from Trinity College Oxford. Louise met him when he was first appointed by the Queen in 1866. But he was dismissed in 1870 as soon as the Queen became aware of her daughter's interest in the poor fellow. The reasons for this were not explained, and so Duckworth's future ecclesiastical career was not affected (he became Vicar of St. Mark's, St. Marylebone and later Canon of Westminster).

Duckworth also appears in another footnote to history: he is identified as Duck in *Alice in Wonderland* and was in fact in the boat in which one summer day in 1862, Lewis Carroll first related the celebrated story of a girl's adventures down a rabbit hole. Indeed, as Duckworth subsequently reported[24], '...the story was actually composed and spoken *over my shoulder* for the benefit of Alice Liddell, who was acting as *cox* of our gig.'

The royal biographical circle was closed[25] by Prince Leopold, Helena's brother, who fell in love with *Alice* Liddell when he went up to Oxford in 1872.

Outside the royal household, Ruland's name first appears on a document discovered in the late 1950s among a pile of old papers in the proverbial attic of King's College London[26]. It is in the form of a letter dated at Windsor on December 17, 1860, i.e., about a year and a half after Ruland's appointment as Prince Consort's Librarian at Windsor. The letter is addressed to Sir Charles Wheatstone FRS, a distinguished figure in Victorian scientific and social circles, and famous for his invention (with Sir William Fothergill Cooke) of the electric telegraph the Victorian equivalent of the Internet.

Wheatstone was professor of experimental physics at King's. Indeed he was the *first* professor of the subject *in the world*, so that it was natural for Ruland to write to him on behalf of Prince Albert as follows (the original is in the Archives of King's College):

Sir,

I am commanded by His Royal Highness the Prince Consort, to draw your attention to the following matter.

The Prince in common with everyone to whom the progress of our telegraphic communications as one of the great civilising agents of the day, is of great importance, has often reflected upon the unsatisfactory results obtained by our submarine cables, which have from their construction hitherto baffled all exertions to establish long deep-sea communications. The bulk and weight of the cables, the want of elasticity, the difficulty of transporting them and spinning them out, and perhaps above all the difficulty of their manufacture on account of the incongruity of the many different substances of which they are composed together with the great pressure exercised by the water upon them, - may be looked upon as some of the most essential causes of failure.

In reflecting upon, how some of these might be overcome, the idea suggested itself to His Royal Highness, whether

> water itself could not be used as the conducting medium? A simple tube of caoutchouc, such as our flexible gas-tubes, might enclose and isolate a column of water, through which the spark might be sent. It would be cheap of manufacture, homogeneous in material, flexible, light, and the outward pressure would be neutralised as the fluid inside would be the same as that outside.
>
> There may occur to you a thousand reasons, why this idea cannot be practically carried out; but His Royal Highness thought you would forgive the trouble if he asked you, who stands in such a parental position to our telegraph-system, to let his Royal Highness have your opinion upon it.
>
> I am, Sir,
> Your obedient servant
> (signed) *C. Ruland*
> Librarian

Strenuous attempts have been made to discover what Sir Charles' reply was, but without success. There is, strangely, no trace of it among Prince Albert's papers, which are said to have been 'dispersed'. However, the *Wheatsone Papers* at King's College contain a clue to what Wheatstone's reply might have been. Wheatstone calculated that a tube 9 feet in internal diameter, filled with seawater, would be necessary as a replacement for a copper wire one-sixteenth of an inch in diameter. That seems to have been the end of the matter.

The transatlantic cable was laid in 1866, six years after the Prince's letter was received.

Ruland's letter on behalf of Prince Consort demonstrates that the Prince was not only very well informed, but was also capable of posing some pretty penetrating questions on topics in science and technology. To what extent these were truly his own questions is impossible to tell.

A very perceptive observer, the distinguished Victorian mathematician and friend of Wheatstone's, Ada Lovelace, provided an interesting sidelight on this in a letter to her husband, written many years earlier from that splendid house that still stands in London's St. James' Square[27]. She told him that Wheatstone regarded Prince Albert as a 'very clever young man' and that this was also the opinion of 'other first rate men of science in Germany'. The prince was very keen to be at the head of a scientific circle in England and was mortified at 'the opposition and cold water .... thrown on all his desires in this respect ..... [The] Prince wants .... a sensible advisor and suggester, to indicate to him the channels for his exercising a scientific influence. ...... He is very clever .... but in a slow way; not a brilliant man.'

It may be that the letter to Wheatstone was the eventual result of all this. At any rate it is refreshing - or at least interesting - to see comments about the Royal family that emanate from external sources and are not entirely based, as is most often the case, on Royal family letters and journals, and, of course, their former employees.

Ruland's major task in the service of Prince Albert was, however, something quite different. It was a project that he took over in 1859, on his appointment as Librarian in succession to Dr. Ernest Becker; it ensured that his name became part - albeit a small one - of the vocabulary of the history of art.

The project is outlined in an article entitled *The Raphael Collection of H.R.H. the Prince Consort,* which was published[28] in 1863. Its authors - Becker and Ruland - are described as *formerly librarians to H.R.H.*

The plan was formulated towards the end of 1852 and work began in the following February. The Prince's novel idea was to assemble a collection of photographic *reproductions* of old masters, which could then be made available to students of art and of the history of art.

The Royal collection at Windsor Castle as it was left by King George III contained a great many significant items, and it soon became clear that the scope of Prince Albert's plan was too wide and that, at least to begin with, the collection would have to be restricted to only one major artist. The Prince chose Raphael as the first famous figure to be represented in the proposed collection, and directed the efforts of his assistants towards the assembly of reproductions of the works of the Umbrian master. This choice had the advantage that an introduction to the work of Raphael was already available in the form of a monograph by J. D. Passavant, entitled *Raphael von Urbino* and published in 1839.

The effort devoted to this enterprise can be appreciated by inspecting the three volumes of correspondence deposited in the Department of Prints and Drawings of the British Museum (a detailed account is given by Jennifer Montagu in her article *The Ruland/Raphael Collection*[29]).

Of course, the work of Becker and Ruland was greatly facilitated by the unique status of the Prince Consort throughout Europe (Becker, and later Ruland, wrote on his behalf to the curators of every major collection). It was also greatly helped by developments in photography, which was barely past its infancy and revolutionised the art of reproduction (and *vice versa*). It was probably Ernest Becker, a founder member of the London Photographic Society, who originally introduced Prince Albert to photography, and this interest was subsequently pursued by other members of the Royal Family[30].

The principal collections that were photographed were those in Oxford University (140 items), the Woodburn Collection (about 70), the collection in Accademia di belli Arti in Venice (101), Prince Esterhazy's Collection in Vienna (88), the Louvre Collection in Paris (50) and several others. The only person who refused permission to photograph was a Miss Woodburn who feared that photography would reduce the 'value of her treasure', but after some pressure she eventually relented.

Even now, as Jennifer Montagu points out, 'there is no assemblage of [Raphael's] works anywhere that can rival the collection brought together by the efforts of the Prince Consort'. The entire collection is now on indefinite loan to the British Museum in

Carl Ruland in the 1880s

London, whose catalogue of Italian drawings in the Department of Prints and Drawings by P. Pouncey and J.A. Gere describes it as being of 'unique value'.

The final outcome of all this work was the catalogue entitled *The Works of Raphael Santi da Urbino as Represented in The Raphael Collection in the Royal Library at Windsor Castle, formed by H.R.H. The Prince Consort, 1853-1861 and Completed by Her Majesty Queen Victoria.* It was printed, in a limited edition of 100 copies[31], in Weimar in 1876 (by which time Ruland had permanently returned to Germany). It includes a twenty-page *Introduction* by Ruland and is often colloquially referred to as the *Ruland Catalogue.*

Ruland thus became well-known as a Raphael scholar. For example, in England he was asked to produce, among other things, *Notes on the Cartoons of Raphael now in the South Kensington Museum, and on Raphael's Other Works* (published by Her Majesty's Stationary Office in 1867). He also wrote the introduction to the 1887 catalogue of Ad. Braun and Company of Paris and Dornach, who were the official publishers of photographs of works of art to a number of national museums (Adolphe and Gaston Braun made significant contributions to the photography of Old Masters).

Ruland was eventually appointed director of the newly-founded Grand-Ducal Museum in Weimar (in 1870) and director of its successor, the Goethe National Museum in Weimar (in 1884). But he continued his work on the Raphael catalogue and made return visits from Weimar until it was finally published in 1876.

Carl Ruland died in Weimar on November 13, 1907. A son, C. F. Ruland, died in Leipzig in 1946, having passed on to his god-daughter, a Mrs. Strosyk, the collection of personal letters written by Princess Helena to his father and a few simple sketches. It has not been possible to discover precisely how and why Mrs. Strosyk's son eventually passed them on to the Royal Archives in Windsor[32].

The involvement of Carl Ruland in the princess' teenage years was a profound event in her life. It is likely that Ruland influenced her in her choice of books for translation from German. He certainly advised her sister Alice on the history of art in the 1870s and so he may well have advised Helena in her work on the Margravine of Baireuth in the 1880s.

Placid, plump, dowdy and ...?

In her *Journal* and her *Letters*, Queen Victoria was often unkind in her references to her third daughter Helena, and others have generally followed her example (of course, one does not know the content of the pages that were burnt on her instructions by Princess Beatrice, her literary executor, after the Queen's death).

At the same time, one is really hard put to it to find something *really* unflattering about Queen Victoria herself or her children on the innumerable pages of memoirs and letters produced by the 'royal writings industry' and that hard-working 'sub-species, the Royal biographer'.

The number of people who have written about the Royal Family, even before some of the more recent events, is enormous. It seems that every flunkey, civil servant and aristocrat who has ever come into contact with Queen Victoria, however remotely, has written a book or long article about it. And the published pages have been largely devoid of serious criticism of the diminutive, but heavy Queen.

This inevitably raises a simple question: can her *Letters* and *Journal*, and the writings of her friends, relatives and employees be really taken at their face value? For example, anyone reading the biographical sketch and letters entitled *Alice - Grand Duchess of*

Hesse[33] would not be aware of a major row that exploded between Alice - Helena's older sister - and their mother. It was to do with the Queen's marriage plans for Helena.

Teenage photograph of Helena

In 1863, the Queen began to be preoccupied with Helena's future - as usual, in the context of her own plans. On May 18, 1863 - when Helena was 17 - Victoria wrote as follows to one of her favourite people, namely, her uncle King Leopold of Belgium whom she regarded as a kind of father figure[34]: 'A married daughter I MUST have living with me, and must not be left constantly to look about for help.... I intend (and she wishes it herself) to look out in a year or two (for till nineteen or twenty I don't intend *she* should marry) for a young sensible Prince, for Lenchen to marry, who can during MY *lifetime* make my house his *principal* home. Lenchen is so useful, and her whole character so well adapted to live in the house, that ..... I could *not* give her up without *sinking* under the weight of my desolation. A sufficient fortune to live independently if I died, and plenty of good sense and high moral worth are the only necessary requisites'.

As she appears in her teens, Helena is often presented - especially by her mother - in terms of descriptors such as *placid, plump, dowdy, uncomplicated, unambitious, obedient, without charm* ...... Of course, her entire education, was closely supervised by her parents and was impressed by a number of governesses. It was surprisingly liberal and included instruction in serious subjects as well as in 'accomplishments' and domestic arts. She was expected to become (and indeed did become) fluent in French and German.

The whole thing was an execution of a master plan devised by the Prince Consort on the basis of a proposal put forward by his close adviser and former tutor Baron Christian Stockmar in a document entitled *Memorandum on the Education of the Royal Children*. The document was submitted[35] on March 6, 1842 and the problem was examined further in another memorandum submitted on July 28, 1846, soon after Princess Helena was born.

Although Stockmar's prescription was mainly focussed on the education of the heir to the throne and the Princess Royal, it nevertheless contained some basic principles which, whilst defining what may be called *Victorianism*, do not altogether conform to modern stereotypes of the Victorian era[36].

Stockmar recommended starting as early as possible a strict regime designed to impart discipline, erudition and high moral tone, whilst at the same time emphasizing 'freedom of thought' as well as 'laws of morality'.

The high tone of the words and phrases in the Stockmar memoranda did not in fact suit the young (and, later, the older) Prince of Wales, and indeed turned out to be more of a prescription for keeping up appearances, which in the end was easily interpreted as *hypocrisy* by those unsympathetic to Stockmar's prescription.

Whatever the theoretical value of these principles of education, in practice the royal children did acquire a respect for learning and intellectual pursuits; in the end, they all became 'genuine progressives' and were prevented by their education and upbringing from becoming mere royal nonentities[37].

On the purely practical side, the new feature of the bringing up of the royal children was the direct close involvement of the Queen and the Prince Consort in the life of their children: they were not in their early years removed to an isolated nursery and left there to the staff hired for the purpose. On the contrary, there was constant intervention, observation and comment from the royal parents. The downside was that mother became the overwhelmingly dominant figure in the life of these children, which became oppressive as they grew older.

In succeeding years, it was easier for Helena's sisters Alice and Vicky to reach a state of relative independence. They eventually detached themselves physically from their mother's immediate sphere of influence, the former by marrying Louis, the Grand Duke of Hesse-Darmstadt, and the latter by marrying the German Crown Prince (later Emperor Frederick III).

Helena, on the other hand, was never to be more than a walk or a short drive away from her powerful and anxious mother. For much of the time in later years she was constantly at her beck and call, and she eventually became a kind of super-secretary-cum-companion to the Queen.

There is some evidence that she tried to resist - or at least delay - her very time consuming attachment as companion to the Queen. Thus, she continued to offer the view that it would be desirable to allow her sister Princess Louise to consider a number of suitors before she accepted any of them. It was suspected that this was a delaying tactic because Helena - who after her marriage lived in the nearby Frogmore House - would be the next person in line to assume the responsibility of a companion to the Queen (Beatrice was still too young)[38]. A husband as good looking and as clever as that provided by the Duckworth model was difficult to find for Louise, but the Queen eventually put up the Marquis of Lorne, 9th Duke of Argyll, and Louise accepted and married him.

As we shall see, it is something of a miracle that the dutiful Princess Helena, who eventually did become her mother's companion and secretary, managed, despite all the impedimenta placed in her way, to achieve so many remarkable successes.

The first step - after all the previous difficulties were overcome - was to find a suitable husband for Lenchen. The Queen was still in seemingly indefinite deep mourning after the death of Prince Albert in 1861, but certain things could not be postponed, among them the search for a suitable husband for Lenchen. But her mother made it quite clear: 'I must have Lenchen with me for the greater part of the year when she is married, and this she knows....'

The first tentative measures were taken by evaluating two or three possible candidates in the form of continental princes in 1863. Among those that came to England were Henry of Hesse, the brother of Prince Louis, the husband of Princess Alice. The brothers of the Princess of Wales came from Denmark, and the Prince of Orange arrived from Holland. Contemporary documents[39] reveal all kinds of machinations and intensive lobbying from a number of directions.

One of the first suggestions was put forward by Helena's sister Vicky, the Crown Princess of Prussia. She proposed Prince Albert (Abbat) of Prussia, a close cousin of her husband's, the Crown

Prince. Abbat was exceedingly rich, and physically and intellectually attractive, and was at first proposed for Princess Louise. However, there was a parallel plan, originally devised by the Prince Consort in a memorandum - written just before he died - to link Abbat to Princess Helena.

Two basic difficulties stood in the way of this idea. First, the Queen wanted her future son in law to reside most of the time in England, so that Helena could continue to work as her companion and secretary. This particular Prussian prince was unlikely to accept such a scheme (actually, he had not even met Helena whilst the exchange of ideas between the Queen and her eldest daughter via Ernest Stockmar and General Grey, her secretary, was going on). Secondly, even if the hypothetical departure of Helena to Berlin to marry Abbat there were to be approved, it was not considered satisfactory in Germany to have *two* of Queen Victoria's daughters in position great influence at the hart of Prussia.

Vicky tried very hard and got her secretary, Ernest Stockmar (son of Christian), to present a closely argued case to General Grey, but eventually gave up when the Queen put up a virtual palisade of objections and initially would not even meet the young man for the fear that he might remove Helena from the orbit around her. And Ernest Stockmar continued to point out that there was an internal contradiction in the Queen's attitude.

On the one hand, she wanted prospective suitors to agree to her conditions but on the other, she would not agree to these potential suitors being told that they were in the running. 'I could not see him' - the Queen wrote to Vicky on June 17, 1863 when it was suggested that Albrecht wanted to come to England. '......... The worry, anxiety and distress this has caused me, have made me quite ill. .... I trust [the visit] may yet be stopped'. On June 29 she insisted that 'Lenchen has seen no one and will see no one'. And yet only a month later Abbat did come to Osborne and was invited to lunch[40].

It is possible - perhaps probable - that the Queen suspected Vicky of making these suggestions because she was trying to capture her younger sister as an assistant for herself, which would certainly have been highly disapproved of by the Queen (and, what's more, '...... Papa over and over objected to that'[41]).

At the same time, there was a strong counter-current of opinion that the possible departure of Helena to Berlin would be a good thing because it would be preferable for the Queen to have a *male* assistant. For example, it was suggested that Prince Alfred could take up this position, but this would require an adjustment of his programme of education and could not be introduced without extensive consultation with ministers because of the extreme sensitivity of the post[42].

While all this was going on, everyone was trying to avoid 'unsettling the mind of the princess'[43] by keeping her in the dark about their plans for her. But it would be very surprising if she had not had a pretty good idea about what was happening, especially since, as her mother's secretary, she was privy to many of the things that crossed her mother's desk.

In the end, these machinations came to nothing. Albrecht had no wish to marry (and may not have known exactly what was going on), the Queen was fearful of losing her daughter and it became clear that the proposed (or, strictly speaking, unproposed) alliance was not a practical idea. The trap laid for the Queen by the two Stockmars did not work.

When it came to a decision, no amount of German logic, whether it came from the Stockmars or the Prussian Crown Prince and Princess, would overcome the Queen's instincts: she did not *really* want Abbat. Old Baron Stockmar could only warn: 'If through her fault the project comes to nothing, she will repent of it - for it will not be easy to find another person who combines in so happy a manner so many of the essential qualities' (quoted in a letter by his son Ernest on March 30, 1863[44]). But in this case at any rate he was wrong.

The next candidate to be considered was Prince Elimar of Oldenburg. He too was suggested by Vicky (after the Abbat episode was over). And again there were letters going backwards and forwards between Ernest Stockmar in Prussia and General Grey in

Windsor, not to mention direct letters between the Queen and her daughters in Germany[45].

In the end, Elimar was invited to Balmoral and arrived there on Tuesday, September 19, 1864, 'His Ducal Highness Prince Elimar of Oldenburg attended by Baron Vultzburg [sic] arrived at the castle on a visit to Her Majesty' - reported the *London Illustrated* on October 1. Both Elimar and Edmund Würtzburg were students at Bonn University and were fascinated by the goings on at the English court.

On Wednesday of that week the Queen drove to the Lynn of Dee accompanied by Princess Helena, Prince Alfred and Prince Elimar. The following day, the same company drove to Alt na Guithasack and the Lynn of Muich. And finally on Thursday, the Queen and the young duo drove to Invercauld. There the princess and the prince were able to exchange words in semi-private by riding ahead of the rest of the little expedition. But on Saturday the two visitors took their leave of the Royal Family and left the castle for Inverness. From there they went to London where they spent a fortnight before returning to Germany. Before they left, General Grey made sure that the young Baron accompanying the Prince promised to write and tell the Queen's private secretary what was the net result of their visit.

Two months later, Edmund Würtzburg wrote to Grey on 'the matter of Prince Elimar and proposed alliance'[46]. He reported that he had 'gained the firm conviction from all [he] could make out and from different occasional remarks ..... that [Prince Elimar] has no intention whatever towards the proposed alliance. He never mentioned the name of the Princess'. Würtzburg went on to make it clear that the Prince was nevertheless aware of what was being suggested, but this was entirely against his 'plans and projects'. And so Helena was turned down again - something her mother tried hard to avoid by her maneuvering with 'conditions' and not inviting people or telling them anything directly, and so on.

Meanwhile, the Queen decided that Helena's prestige could be enhanced by taking some of the Queen's Drawing Rooms. Accordingly, Helena deputised for her mother at the end of May 1865.

A Drawing Room was a splendid affair at which a great many of the Queen's loyal subjects were normally presented to the Queen. Amidst great pomp and circumstance Helena played the part of the Queen very successfully. She was to repeat this success some 35 years later, by which time the Queen found it very difficult to perform her public duties and Helena had become a popular figure.

The final candidate that emerged as a result of the Queen's search - of which Lenchen allegedly knew nothing - was a 35-year old impoverished German whose name was Prince Christian of Schleswig-Holstein-Sonderburg-Augustenburg (it used to be said that the longer the title the smaller the territory). He was closer in age to the Queen than to her daughter and there was therefore some speculation at first that he might have been after the former rather than the latter.

Prince Christian's candidature was introduced by Victoria's uncle Leopold, the interestingly extrovert King of the Belgians, and again by Vicky and her husband Fritz, the German Crown Prince. This immediately gave rise to fierce opposition from all Victoria's children for a variety of different reasons. To understand them, we must quickly glance at the history of two small duchies with the Ruritanian-sounding names of Schleswig and Holstein.

There was nothing very romantic about them. Indeed, the two duchies had a very tortuous and tragic history, which became the source of some ridicule because of its very complexity. For example, Lord Palmerston once famously joked that the Schleswig-Holstein question was more intricate than the riddle of the Sphinx and more difficult to undo than the Gordian knot. It divided itself into two branches: the one about Holstein, the other about Schleswig. In letters to her ambassador in Denmark, the Queen was said to have written about the latter whereas her ambassador replied about the former. Or, to put it yet another way (there is no shortage of jokes on this matter), Palmerston is also reported to have said that only three people understood the Schleswig-Holstein problem: the Prince Consort who was dead, a German professor who had become unreachably insane and Palmerston himself, but he had forgotten the true explanation.

Schleswig and Holstein lay just south of Denmark, in that order. The two duchies became the dominions of Denmark under the Treaty of London of 1852. Schleswig had a large Danish population and Holstein was more German and remained a member of the German Confederation (or Bund).

There were several claimants to the two duchies: The King of Denmark who was Princess (later Queen) Alexandra's father, the King of Prussia (and, therefore, Bismarck) and Duke Frederick of Augustenburg who was supported by a number of the smaller German states who were not on the best of terms with Prussia, to put it mildly.

The population mix and the strategic importance of access to the North Sea were at the basis of the inevitable dispute between Germany (which consisted of thirty eight states until 1886 when Bismarck began the process of unification) and Denmark. In fact, Prussia, the major component of the German Confederation, joined with Austria to defeat the much smaller Denmark, with Austria taking Schleswig and Prussia acquiring Holstein after an ultimatum was put to Denmark to give up its claims. By power plotting and drawing in Italy to press Austria in the south, Bismarck eventually managed to annex both duchies. In the process, Prince Christian of Schleswig-Holstein, like his older brother the Duke Frederick (one of the claimants to the duchies), was stripped not only of his commission in the Prussian Army, but of all his possessions and territories as well.

Engagement photograph of Helena and Christian

Christian was a close friend of the Crown Prince and Princess (Vicky) of Prussia and stayed with them frequently, which was the origin of the suggestion by Vicky that he could be a suitable consort for her sister Helena. She described him in a letter to her mother as 'the best creature in the world' although not as clever as his brother Fritz Augustenburg. This advice was taken very seriously by the Queen.

However, others disagreed vehemently. First, Helena's other sister, Alice, did not like her mother's plotting and was generally against arranged marriages (especially when they were arranged partly for the benefit of the Queen). Second, Alice understood that a marriage between a daughter of the Queen of England and the brother of a claimant to Schleswig and Holstein would be - and actually was - seen in Germany as an insult to Bismarck who had downgraded the Augustenburgs to minimal status and would not allow them to re-emerge. And yet here was Victoria intending to allow a royal Princess to marry someone who in Bismarck's eyes was now effectively a nobody.

Bertie, the Prince of Wales and his wife Alexandra, originally Princess of Denmark, naturally saw Christian as an 'enemy' (because his brother Frederick was a claimant in opposition to the Danish king), but Christian was close to the Prussian Crown Prince and Princess who strongly backed him.

The rift became quite deep and relations were beginning to break down between Alice and her mother, with Alexandra threatening to boycott the potential wedding. However, they finally had to call a truce and all her nine children joined the Queen on a visit to Coburg in August 1865 to unveil a statute to Prince Albert and, taking advantage of the opportunity, for everyone (including Lenchen) to meet Prince Christian.

The Queen had him to lunch and found him 'extremely pleasing, gentlemanlike, quiet and distinguished'. She also recorded her view that Lenchen found him amiable and agreeable.

In September the Queen told Vicky that the whole matter was more or less settled in her own mind and that Helena was 'pleased' about the possibility of an engagement.

In October, the Queen finally concluded in a letter to Augusta (Empress William I of Germany) that 'in Prince Christian ... we have found the right husband. .... Though naturally no engagement has taken place, and cannot take place till they know each other better, yet I may regard the matter as pretty well settled'[47].

By the following January, the Queen began to think about physical realities[48]: Christian smoked cigars almost non-stop and 'looked well but coughing'. She therefore decided to 'see to Christian's teeth and cough'. She also noted[49] that Christian celebrated his birthday in January 1866 and commented '....Alas! his 35th. If only he looked a little younger! .... and his manners and movements are so old. It is such a pity.' She got her doctor and dentist to assist. At least she was being practical.

She peremptorily dismissed all hostile gossip which she was told was circulating in England, including one which claimed that

Christian was a lunatic and the father of 15 illegitimate children, one of whom would be coming to live with him.

Smoking was a serious problem because the Queen strongly objected to the habit. She even disliked receiving letters from people who smoked because paper readily absorbs tobacco smoke. Indeed no-one was allowed to smoke at Osborne House. At first, a special room was built in the garden, but later smoking was allowed in the billiards room. At Windsor, smoking was also allowed in the billiard room (located at some distance from the drawing room), but not elsewhere. And at Balmoral a special room was allocated to smokers near the servants' quarters[50].

While the preparations for Helena's wedding were going on, the Queen was describing her daughter in increasingly more favourable terms. This was a clear change from the more usual '...Lenchen's features are again now so very large and long that it spoils her looks', '....difficulties with her figure', '...does not improve in her looks', 'cannot help her looks'[51].

Helena's last birthday before her marriage was celebrated in the Orangery at Windsor (it was also the first such celebration since her father's death). The event took the form of a tea dance for the children of servants. The dance continued until twenty to eight after which the Royal children joined the Queen for dinner at which a toast to Helena's health was proposed by Princess Beatrice at Helena's 'last birthday at home'. And she was about to lose a highly prized privilege (there weren't too many): it was the honour of sharing the sleeping saloon with the Queen on the Royal train on journeys to Scotland[52].

A few weeks before her marriage, Helena and her great friend Louisa Knightley drove around Virginia Water and talked about the forthcoming marriage. It was probably the nearest Helena came to a real heart to heart discussion. Louisa observed to her diary that Helena spoke 'in simplest and most natural way of her affection for Prince Christian'. Love was not mentioned.

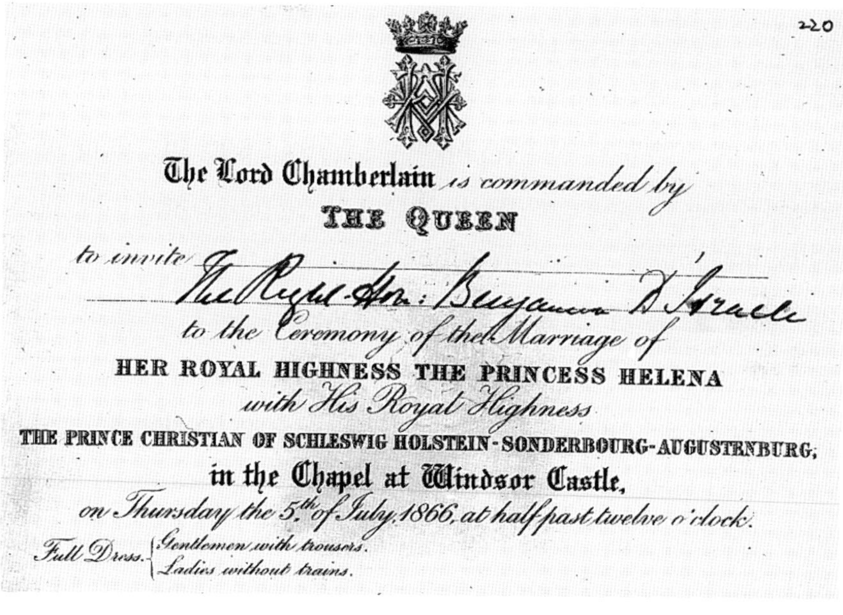

220

The Lord Chamberlain is commanded by

THE QUEEN

to invite The Right Hon: Benjamin D'Israeli

to the Ceremony of the Marriage of

HER ROYAL HIGHNESS THE PRINCESS HELENA

with His Royal Highness

THE PRINCE CHRISTIAN OF SCHLESWIG HOLSTEIN-SONDERBOURG-AUGUSTENBURG,

in the Chapel at Windsor Castle,

on Thursday the 5th of July, 1866, at half past twelve o'clock.

Full Dress. { Gentlemen with trousers. Ladies without trains.

The wedding invitation

Helena married Christian in the private chapel of Windsor Castle on Thursday, July 5, 1866. The chapel was about a hundred yards from the Queen's private apartments in the Victoria Tower and just behind the eastern end of St. George's Hall. Helena was the only one of the Queen's children to be married there. Everything went smoothly, but it was an awkward apartment in which to marshal and arrange a distinguished assembly[53].

A very large wedding party left Paddington for Windsor in a special train. The station was full of men in colourful uniforms and ladies in full evening dress. The train was crowded with celebrities, Disraeli and Gladstone among them. The defeat of the Austrians by Prussia was in everyone's mind as the drama of the royal wedding was unfolding contrapunctually against political drifts in Europe.

Louisa Knightley's report[54] of the wedding provided all the details of the great event. She was up early in her wedding clothes on the Paddington train. Louisa and her friends soon found seats in a compartment of the special train, with Disraeli and Lord Everseley in the next.

The streets of Windsor were gaily decorated as they drove up to the Grand Entrance and marched through St. George's Hall to the top of the equerries' staircase where they were shown into the White Drawing-room and found themselves sitting opposite the whole of the ex-ministry. Lord Derby, General Peel and Benjamin Disraeli were the only representatives of the new Cabinet.

A flourish of trumpets and a grand march announced the approach of the Royal Family in a procession headed by the Maharajah in gorgeous Indian array. After a pause, a burst of martial strains heralded the bridegroom's approach.

Soon the bride advanced slowly, with flushed cheeks and eyes bent on the ground, looking very handsome. The Queen and the Prince of Wales supported her, and her train was borne by eight bridesmaids.

At the solemn service the two 'I wills' rang out loud and clear, the Queen gave her daughter away ('the Queen is plain and not graceful' Louisa noted) and a new life began for the twenty-year old princess.

And Louisa's final verdict on the bridegroom was: 'pre-eminently sensible - the very thing for her generous, impetuous nature, - and he is extremely kind-hearted, and most universally liked.'

The Queen's decision to give her daughter away at the wedding ceremony was unusual if not unique. She justified it on the grounds that as Sovereign she did the work of a man, and giving her daughter away was no different from this point of view. But she continued having little digs at Christian.

Throughout and before the celebrations the Queen 'wished he looked younger, for he really looks older than dear Papa did at 42.....' However, Helena herself seems to have had no doubts. In a letter to Lady Augusta Stanley[55] she wrote 'I am intensely happy...... he is noble, generous, loving and such tact and discretion, never shrinking from saying what he thinks fit......'. And at the ceremony itself, Helena's trusted friend Lady Knightley described[56] the bridegroom as having 'a manly presence and an open face, younger and better-looking than his photos lead one to expect'.

On the morning of the wedding day, the Queen breakfasted alone with Helena. There was a lot of bustle and excitement while Helena dressed in the Queen's bedroom. Outside the private rooms, there were people everywhere.

Before the wedding, Christian formally applied (as late as June 4, 1866) to the Home Secretary for British nationality. In the application, he describes himself[57] as 'having at present no settled place of residence in the United Kingdom'! At more or less the same time, the official *Gazette*[58] carried on its pages the following announcement:

> "The Queen has been pleased to declare and ordain that His Serene Highness Prince Frederick Christian Charles of Schleswig-Holstein-Sonderburg-Augustenburg shall henceforth upon all occasions whatsoever be styled and called His Royal Highness before his name, and such titles as now do, and hereafter may, belong to him; and to command that the said Royal concession and declaration be registered in Her Majesty's College of Arms. The Queen has also been pleased to appoint his Royal Highness Prince Frederick Christian Charles Augustus of Schleswig-Holstein to be Major-General in the Army".

The wedding was celebrated in Windsor town as a general holiday[59] 'in compliment to the amiable Princess, who is so universal a favourite'. The streets of the town were gaily decorated and the Eton boys cheered[60] the couple as they departed for their honeymoon, which was spent on a tour of Paris, Interlaken and Genoa[61].

After the wedding, Prince Christian was rewarded by the Queen with the Garter and the appointment as Ranger of Windsor Great Park. The Queen gave her daughter the use of Frogmore House, a minor Royal residence with extensive grounds - half a mile or so south of Windsor Castle - which had been in Royal ownership since the times of Henry VIII.

And all this happened against the background of historic changes in Europe. The Austro-Prussian war, the battle of Sadowa-Königgratz, the dissolution of the Germanic Confederation and the rise of Prussia in supremacy, all occurred in the summer of 1866. These events were to have a profound effect not only on the future life together of the newlyweds, but also on the future of European nations.

But there were also much more mundane problems for the newlyweds, which had to be attended to, bearing in mind that neither had a significant private income to support them in their married state. Before it was finally settled, the matter was thoroughly gone into in a memorandum filed with correspondence between Sir

George Grey, the Home Secretary at the time, and General Charles Grey, the Queen's private secretary[62].

The finances of the Christians were founded on monies extracted with the help of advice from General Grey by Helena's mother from the House of Commons. For five years after Prince Consort's death in 1861 the Queen had avoided public appearances, much to the displeasure of her subjects, but on February 6, 1866 she came very nervously before Parliament to announce: 'I have recently declared My Consent to a Marriage between My Daughter Princess Helena and Prince Christian of Schleswig Holstein Sonderbourg Augustenbourg [there was always a problem with the spelling of some of these names]. I trust this Union may be prosperous and happy'. She asked for a dower and an annuity for Princess Helena.

The Resolution put to Parliament read: 'That the annual sum of Six Thousand Pounds be granted to Her Majesty, out of the Consolidated Fund of Great Britain and Ireland, the said Annuity to be settled on Her Royal Highness the Princess Helena Augusta Victoria for her life, in such a manner as Her Majesty shall think proper, and to commence from the date of the Marriage of Her Royal Highness with Prince Christian....' The annuity was 'free of all taxes'. A dower of £30,000 was also asked for. The eventual Act of Parliament was dated March 23, 1866.

The Chancellor of the Exchequer, who moved the Resolution explained that, to avoid misunderstanding, it had to be recalled that on accession of each succeeding Sovereign, he or she surrenders life interests of Crown Estates whilst a sufficient provision is made by Parliament for the maintenance of the Royal household and establishment. However, this did not include that which related to the making of 'competent provision for the members of the family as they come to adult age and go out into the world'. All this devolved upon the Government and Parliament, who had to consider each case separately.

Disraeli's comment on the Resolution, put forward in response to the statement by the Chancellor, is interesting in the light of subsequent events, right up to the present time. He thought that the proposition of the Ministry was 'judicious and well-considered' and went on: 'I think the Chancellor of the Exchequer did right in recalling .... the conditions under which Her Majesty at her succession relinquished her power over the large estates of the Crown. ..... When the Civil List Act was passed ...... I had great doubts as to the policy of that measure, because it occurred to me that when the time arrived that appeals to Parliament by the Crown of this character had to be made, the circumstances under which the original Civil List Act was passed would be forgotten, that Her Majesty would be appealing to a new generation, and the whole character of the Royal claim might be subject to great misinterpretation'. Subsequent history proved him right.

The annuity agreed to by Parliament was lower than Helena's brothers were allowed, but, of course, the Queen herself gave financial support as well. She provided a capital investment of £100,000 which yielded an income of £4,000 per annum[63]. She also gave financial help with the maintenance of Frogmore House and, later, of Cumberland Lodge[64]. After allowing for personal expenses of £2,000 per annum each, and for personal staff at £950 per annum, the budget left £7,000 available for the 'establishment' (their homes - one in Windsor and the other in London - were provided rent and tax free).

Interestingly enough, the Grey papers reveal that Prince Christian himself had an income of only $6,000 per annum (about £1,000 at the time). His wealth - or rather the absence of it - was obviously of no great significance in this connection.

A few months after the wedding, *The Lady's Own Paper* produced the following verdict on Helena's new husband:

> 'We regret that Prince Christian has not been over and above popular in England since his arrival; though we do not see any definite reason for this. It is true certain sinister rumours concerning him have gained currency, more or less, but there does not appear to be any grounds for them. On his coming to England he was well received, and he has done nothing, so far as we know, to forfeit the good esteem that was accorded him.'

This was not untypical of comments in the British press generally and the Prince continued to be held in 'good esteem' thereafter.

Frogmore House and Cumberland Lodge

Frogmore House was Helena's first home of her own. Although her mother's influence was all-pervading, Helena must have had some real room to manouvre because she was allowed to plan the refurbishment of her new home. This must have been successful because her younger sister, Princess Louise, consulted her when she had to redecorate her own house after she married the Duke of Argyll[65].

The Christians' first child, Christian Victor Albert, was born at Frogmore in 1867 ('the most beautiful child I ever saw: such blue eyes, such white flesh, & such manly glance and brow' - reported Disraeli[66] in a letter to his wife in 1868). Two other children - Albert and Victoria Helena - followed in 1869 and 1870, respectively. In 1876, Disraeli described them[67] in a letter from Cumberland Lodge to Lady Chesterfield in very favourable terms: 'I never saw children better brought up; they are engaging -- & they are pretty; I dislike ugly children'.

There is considerable unanimity in contemporary reports about Helena's new husband. As usual, Disraeli struck a typically penetrating note when he told Lady Knightley at dinner in Osborne in 1868 that the Prince 'combined tact with a deep, slow-moving mind' and that 'he was both sensible and good-natured'. In other words, he avoided rocking the boat and did what was expected of him as a satisfactory consort[68]. A few years later, in a letter[69] to Lady Bradford, he expressed a still sharper view by referring to him as '.... the excellent Christian .... a shrewd, sagacious man - slow only in manner and with some sense of humour - a good man.'

On the other hand, as late as May 25, 1872, the Queen was still sending out deprecating messages such as[70] 'Lenchen is 26 today. She looks much older'.

In July 1872 the family moved to Cumberland Lodge in Windsor Great Park, which became their permanent country home. A fourth child, Marie Louise was born there in 1872 and there was also another son, Harold, who survived only nine days in 1876. A stillborn son was recorded at Cumberland Lodge in May 1877.

Cumberland Lodge as it is today

The scale of existence and the degree of comfort in a Royal establishment such as Cumberland Lodge, funded as it was, directly or indirectly, by parliamentary and Royal subventions, is indicated

Princess Christian with her two sons

by the staff employed at the Lodge[71]. While the sons of the Christians went off to board at Wellington and Charterhouse schools, the daughters remaining at home had a German governess and three

Drawing room at Cumberland Lodge at the turn of the century

maids (English, French and German, respectively). Prince Christian had a personal valet. There were also a housekeeper, cook, four housemaids, still room maid, kitchen maid, scullery maid, as well as underbutler, three footmen, underfootman, coal porter, further servants who came in daily, 24 grooms and stablemen, four gardeners, coachman, wheelwright, farrier and farmer. The were other attendees. For example, the Princess had a lady-in-waiting.

The Princess was always very busy with the innumerable charities and institutions that she ran or supported, but the Prince had

Entrance hall at Cumberland Lodge

a very much more leasurely existence. He played with his dog Corrie, he fed his numerous pigeons with peas, he hunted and he did all the things an Englishman of his status should have been doing. One of the results of this activity was that his left eye was shot out by a ricochet bullet fired by his brother in law, Prince Arthur. Thereafter he wore an artificial eye.

He had a set of such eyeballs and one of his party tricks was to take the glass eye out and replace it with another, much to the discomfort of his companions. But in the privacy of his study, he

The Library at Cumberland Lodge in the 1880s

often wore a pair of goggles with a green shield on one side and an open aperture on the other.

The Prince had very little to do. He was High Steward of Windsor and Ranger of Windsor Great Park. Neither of these functions were very onerous. Attempts were therefore made to occupy his time with some other functions. For example, he was made one of the Royal

Commissioners for the Great Exhibition of 1851 (from 1870 onwards) and between 1881 and 1904 he was Chairman of the Management Board of the Commission. Surviving letters[72] to Sir Lyon Playfair show that the Prince wrote in fluent idiomatic English. He could, whenever necessary, express himself in strong language, but always deferred to his royal consort to whom he referred as 'the Princess'. However, the Prince was really a figurehead (frequently absentee figurehead) and the Board was run by Playfair.

The Prince was also occasionally sent by the Queen and, later, by Edward VII, on a number of missions to foreign courts.

His obituarist in the local newspaper in Windsor struggled a bit, but finally came out with the strictly accurate expression 'He was a great huntsman, a skillful shot, a keen agriculturalist and a good pedestrian'. His daughter, Marie Louise recorded in her *Memoirs* that he loved literature, often listened to debates in the House of Commons and became friendly with Benjamin Disraeli.

At Cumberland Lodge, the Christians generally led a comfortable family life with annual holidays being taken at Wolfesgarten, the summer palace of the Grand Duke of Hesse, located in wooded country between Darmstadt and Frankfurt[73].

Occasionally, the Prince acted as an intermediary with the Prussian court. On February 22, 1881 he was spotted in the uniform of a Prussian general among the party greeting the Prince of Wales on his visit to Berlin. The occasion gave rise to an anecdote whereby the

Prince of Wales asked an equerry 'who is that old German general? I'm sure I've seen him before'. The embarrassed equerry had to point out that the general was in fact his brother in law.

Prince Christian's presence there was a sign of a reconciliation with the Hohenzollerns after 20 years of estrangement, cemented by the marriage of Crown Prince William of Prussia on February 27 of that year to Augusta Victoria of Schleswig-Holstein-Sonderburg-Augustenburg, the niece of Prince Christian[74].

This pleasant existence was disrupted in later years by a major tragedy. The Christians, and indeed the entire royal family, were devastated by the loss in 1900 of their eldest son Christian Victor. Like many others, he died of enteric fever whilst serving with the 60th Rifles in the South African War.

Helena responded with typical practicality: she commissioned a biography of her son[75], had it published by John Murray and established a memorial to him in Windsor. It survives there in modified form as the H.R.H. Princess Christian's Hospital. There is also a statue of Christian Victor (unveiled by Lord Roberts in 1904) just outside the walls of Windsor Castle. It was designed by the Windsor architect A. Y. Nutt who was also responsible for the memorial in the cathedral churchyard in Pretoria[76].

The prince was a 'keen and thorough soldier, ... although a strict disciplinarian, he was much loved by his men'.[77]

Princess Christian in South Africa

The Princess' interest in South Africa is commemorated by the fact that the very large number of islands on the Zambezi includes three islands named after Princess Christian and her two daughters Marie Louise and Victoria Helena, respectively. They mark their visits to Southern Africa, especially the visit of Princess Christian in 1904.

Prince Christian Victor

The Princess' other son, Albert, was something of a disappointment to her and her family. The elder brother of Prince Christian, who had no children, offered to make Albert his heir if his parents would allow Albert to adopt German nationality. The parents agreed and Albert eventually succeeded his uncle as Duke of Schleswig-Holstein (in 1921). There was great embarrassment when Albert joined the German Army in World War I although he is said to have steadfastly refused to take part in active service against his mother's country (before that he had been an officer in the Kaiser's bodyguard[78]).

Thereafter Albert became a historical non-entity in the annals of the British Royal Family and obvious reminders of him were carefully removed from public places. For example, his banner of the Order of the Bath was removed from Westminster Abbey, but the authorities there have no knowledge of what happened to it (one authoritative source has suggested that the banner is 'probably somewhere in a cupboard').

Although Albert was unmarried when he died in 1931, an illegitimate daughter of his appeared in the 1930s in the shape of a Mrs. Valerie Wagner, later Duchess d'Arenberg. Valerie Marie, who was born on April 3, 1900 in Liptovsky-Svaty Mikulas, Hungary, was beautiful and rich after her second marriage, and was much loved by Helena's daughter Marie Louise (who mentions her very briefly in her memoirs).

Valerie died on August 14, 1953 in Mont Boron, France[79] (not 1950 as stated by Voules[80]). She is thought to have committed suicide[81]. Edward Voules, who was Marie Louise's constant (but very gay) companion in the 40s and 50s, and must have known all the gossip of the time, corroborates in his memoirs the fact that Valerie's death was the result of a suicide. Further corroboration comes from at least one other informal, but well-informed source.

The circumstances of Valerie's death might be of interest to hunters for the signs of porphyria among the descendants of Queen Victoria because personality changes constitute one of the diagnostic symptoms of the disease, as is amply demonstrated by the well-documented behaviour of George III. The death certificate issued by the local authorities in Nice does not give the cause of death.

Valerie d'Arenberg is an interesting figure. Her mother's name was never revealed by her father (who admitted that she was his daughter just before he died) and Valerie was brought up by Jewish foster parents whose surname was Schwalb. She eventually married Johann Wagner, an Austrian lawyer, in 1935. In 1939 she changed her official name to zu Schleswig-Holstein, thereby declaring the fact that Prince Albert was her father. The marriage to Wagner was annulled by the Catholic Church in 1940, a civil marriage to the tenth Duke of Arenberg having been performed in 1939 after divorce from Wagner in 1938.

A carefully phrased letter witnessed[82] (perhaps even composed) by the distinguished barrister, A.C.B. Webb, and signed in July 1938 by Princess Helena Victoria and Princess Marie Louise, is cited by Marlene Eilers Koenig[83]. The letter confirmed Valerie's antecedents, but it also added: 'Our brother, the Duke of Schleswig-Holstein, in a personal letter to Valerie Wagner, deplored the fact that she had been entrusted to the care of a family of a different race and faith to her own'.

This was enough to make doubly certain that Nazi regulations that forbade marriages between Christians and Jews were not broken. It also adds an unpleasant whiff to the whole story. One wonders what happened to the Schwalbs. And whoever supplied the information cited in the death certificate issued in Nice took care to say that Valerie's mother was a Princess of Schleswig-Holstein. It is unlikely that she was.

There is as yet no evidence that Princess Helena was aware of the existence of her only grandchild, and it is sad that her branch of the family line should end on this dissonant note.

Valerie d'Arenberg had no children. Marie Louise attended her burial at Enghien in Belgium in October 1953, two months after her death. A brief report of the Princess' visit appeared in the local newspaper without mentioning the reasons for it. A purely private affair was kept private.

It was at Cumberland Lodge on July 5, 1916 that the Christians celebrated - uniquely among Queen Victoria's children - their Golden Wedding with a service in the chapel in Windsor Park and a party back at the Lodge

Despite the war that was raging at the time, the German Emperor, William II, sent the Christians 'his loyal and devoted good wishes' via the Crown Princess of Sweden. The subtle penetration of Europe by Queen Victoria's descendants thus continued to bear some fruit even in the extremely difficult circumstances of the World War I.

The German Emperor, the son of Helena's elder sister Vicky and the husband of Augusta Victoria (known as Dona) - the daughter of Prince Christian's brother - was perhaps signalling that he had not forgotten aunt Helena's support when, many years earlier, he was wooing his future wife and was trying to speed up the approval of the proposed marriage[84].

The Prussian establishment of the time was deliberately procrastinating because they regarded Dona as the daughter of a parvenue[85] and not good enough for a future Kaiser (she was actually the grand-daughter of Queen Victoria's half-sister Feodora who had a mere countess as a grandmother!). Perhaps the Kaiser also knew that Helena was kinder to him than he was to many of his English relatives. Indeed she tried to explain his behaviour in terms of 'thoughtlessness' rather than 'premeditation'[86].

But the end of such explicit familial connections was in sight. British public opinion was thought to be unwilling to put up with the transnational cosiness, and all German names such as Schleswig-Holstein were jettisoned and replaced by first names alone. The

British Royal House became the House of Windsor (although, strictly speaking, the British royals could be looked upon as Wettins), Princess Christian of Schleswig-Holstein-Sonderburg-Augustenburg became simply Princess Christian, and their daughters became Princesses Marie Louise and Helena Victoria (effectively *princesses of nothing*, as someone sarcastingly pointed out).

The German connection and the German accents thus vanished from public view, but the sardonic compilers of the so-called *Windsor Alphabet* responded to this change of name with the lines[87]:

> **W** *is for Windsor*
> *our new family name*
> *It sounds terribly British,*
> *but we are Huns just the same.*

The 'alphabet' was allegedly devised by Lord Carisbrooke and his brother Maurice of Battenberg, the sons of Helena's sister Beatrice, the fifth and last daughter of Queen Victoria. But, of course, by then the Kaiser had been displaced by a still more bigoted crew, which in turn led to the German catastrophe of the 1930s and beyond.

All that careful nurturing and supporting that Queen Victoria provided for her daughter Vicky produced an enlightened and talented mother for William, but the final result was an objectionable character in the shape of the last German Kaiser[88].

'A writer of some distinction'

In 1895 the Christians were visited at Cumberland Lodge - their country residence - by what we would now call *a Court Correspondent*, one Mary Spencer-Warren, who called on behalf of the well-known periodical, *The Strand Magazine.* She reported in some detail on the interior of the Lodge and on the interests of the Prince and Princess. She also took some photographs of the house and of the individual rooms.

The house was externally not dissimilar from what it is today: some of the rooms in the Lodge still display traces of the usual heavily elaborate Victorian interiors.

The fact that Prince Christian, not unusually for those days, liked to shoot birds and other animals is clearly indicated in these photographs by a variety of stags' heads mounted on walls.

In the dining room there are pictures by Stubbs. In Princess Christian's room there are collections of ornaments, jewelry and china, but also many bound volumes of music of 'all the best masters', reflecting the Princess' great interest in music.

'As is well known' - the report continues - 'the Princess Christian is devoted to music....... and plays a great deal at home and in concerts and entertainments for the benefit of the poor....' The Princess is said to be a member of the Windsor Madrigal Society, regularly attending the practices. 'She is very active in charitable activities and displays a framed certificate of proficiency in nursing' (she attended, among other things, the Ladies' Classes of the Windsor Centre of the St. John's Ambulance Association)[89].

Spencer-Warren notes the presence of a large collection of books, an indication that the Princess 'is an omnivorous reader'. She is also described by her as 'a writer of some distinction.'

A writer? A writer of what? Well, detailed searches reveal some interesting titles. The first indication of writing talent appears in a preface by Sir Charles Grey to his collection of the early letters of the Prince Consort, published in 1867 and republished several times thereafter. General Grey notes[90] that 'The translations of the Prince's letters......... are for the most part and with a few merely verbal corrections, by Princess Helena. They are made .... with surprising fidelity....'. It is worth remembering that he is referring to a young woman of only 21 or so.

This was the first public indication that the princess had a talent for words. But, first, she had some immediate duties to attend to, namely, those concerned with establishing a home (with the Queen interfering as much as she was allowed to), raising children, working for her mother as a glorified private secretary and attending public engagements on her own and on her mother's behalf.

Her appointments list shows that Princess Christian was a very busy member of the Royal Family at a time when the Royals were not yet expected to attend public functions to the extent they do now. Indeed, it was Princess Christian and Princess Alexandra that were largely responsible for transforming the public duties of the Royals to what they are today. And Princess Christian always maintained a very high profile in the public eye.

But there are clues that behind the stolid and conventional image of the Princess, as cultivated for her by some of her contemporaries and by disinterested historians subsequently, there was a strong, attractive and capable but troubled personality.

She took considerable interest in politics and political figures. The Victorian writer and brilliant political and theological adventurer Laurence Oliphant[91] was a close friend since Helena's childhood. Their friendship was close enough for her to put him up for an extended period in June 1886 at Cumberland lodge when he fell ill with a violent attack of fever.

She also maintained a friendly relationship with Lord Beaconsfield (Benjamin Disraeli). For example, she wrote to Lord Beaconsfield on at least a couple of occasions[92] to introduce Oliphant (who, incidentally, was also well thought of by the Queen, the Prince of Wales and Vicky).

Lord Beaconsfield was a particular favourite of the Princess. In earlier times, Lady Augusta Stanley[93] described Princess Helena as being 'quite mad about politics - for Dizzy and against Gladstone' and 'wild about Dizzy'. Her admiration of Disraeli was also clear from other letters. For example, her close friend Louisa, Lady Knightley refers[94] to correspondence in which Princess Helena is described as 'praising Disraeli's wise, far-seeing conduct'. And in a letter to Sir Theodore Martin some years later she wrote[95]: 'My own fury with Mr. Gladstone & Co. knows no bounds'.

She was not the only lady - young or old - to be overwhelmed with admiration for her mother's great friend. In her letters to Disraeli, she described herself[96] as the recipient of his 'constant kindness towards me since my earliest childhood ... '. Indeed the friendship was so close that Lord Beaconsfield was invited to visit[97] the Christians at Cumberland Lodge in the middle 1870s.

The Princess may have formed an attachment to Dizzy, but her young daughters instantly disliked him[98] and had to be sent out when they found themselves in his company! Perhaps a degree of maturity was necessary before anyone could really appreciate the wit and sagacity of the 'strange old comedian' as Lytton Strachey called him many years later[99].

Unfortunately, whilst Disraeli liked to joke with Helena and her sisters on his regular visits to Windsor, when they were still children, he later had some reservations about visiting the Christians at Cumberland Lodge.

On April 15, 1876 he wrote[100] to Lady Bradford: 'I grieve to say I must, somehow or other, find myself at Cumberland Lodge, Windsor Great Forest, on an Easter visit to their Royal Highnesses the Christians'. But this may have been a reflection of his intense dislike of the cold, snowy weather that dominated that winter. When he finally got there, he was welcomed by Prince Christian, who took him to 'the coldest room I have ever inhabited', although things seemed to improve after tea when he found blazing logs and 'the dear aneroid which had counted 50, was 10 degrees higher'. The cold may have put him off the food provided by his hosts: 'I thought I was safe in depending on lamb and poultry. The lamb could only have been killed yesterday and no barn door would have acknowledged the *volaille*. Curiously tough!...' What with a cold room and disappointing food, he decided to leave a day earlier. But 'the people are kind & good' he told his wife in a letter from the Lodge[101].

In her admiration for Dizzy, Helena followed her mother on whose behalf she wrote[102] to Mrs. Disraeli a few years earlier (in May 1868): '... Mama desires me to ..... send you the accompanying flowers in her name for Mr. Disraeli. She heard him say one day the he was so fond of May and of all those lovely spring flowers that she has ventured to send him these, as they will make his rooms look so bright. The primroses came from Windsor.'

Others received their favourite flowers, but only after they had gone. For example, General Grey the Queen's secretary and close adviser received his - 'lilies of the valley, his favourite flower' - as the Queen's last greeting.

The last gift received by Disraeli from his Sovereign was clearly different - it consisted of primroses; and the inscription on his monument was 'Kings love him that speaketh right'. And yet, after his death, Gladstone enquired[103] of a society lady at dinner: '.... did you ever hear Lord Beaconsfield express particular admiration for primroses? The glorious lily, I think, was much more to his taste.' But he was wrong, and was merely offering sour grapes, for he was referring to a man who, in Maurois' words,[104] was 'a symbol of what can be accomplished in a cold and hostile universe by a long youthfulness of heart'.

Another, and very different, person who stayed with the Christians at Cumberland Lodge (for a month in the autumn of 1880) was Prince William, the future Kaiser and son of Helena's eldest sister Victoria, the Crown Princess of Prussia. He returned to Berlin at the end of November to prepare for his wedding to Princess Augusta Victoria of Schleswig Holstein Sonderburg Augustenburg (Dona), the daughter of Duke Frederick (who 16 years earlier laid claim to the Duchy of Holstein) and therefore a niece of Prince Christian.

When Bismarck was faced with having to give advice on the proposed marriage, he put off the decision as long as possible because of his dislike of the Augustenburgs, but Dona was popular with Queen Victoria and with everyone else, and the marriage took place on February 27, 1881.

Unfortunately, none of this moderated William's mostly bigotted attitude to everyone, including his own mother, although the future Wilhelm II was well aware, especially in later years, of his unbreakable ties to the clan whose head was Queen Victoria - the Grandmama of Europe, or at least of the Royals of Europe[105].

Helena was particularly good with words. It is pretty clear that, in her translations of the relatively daring books that attracted her attention, she took the opportunity - in her introductions - to smuggle in opinions that would elsewhere have caused more than a mere raised eyebrow (and a few strong words from the Queen on whom the Christians depended to some extent for financial support).

When in 1887 she published her translation (from the French) of *The Memoirs of Wilhelmine, Margravine of Baireuth,* the reviews were universally complimentary. *The Times* described the translation as 'admirable' and the book itself as 'most interesting'. *The Saturday Review* noted that the translator 'has given an English version which is thoroughly alive.....In mere dictionary accuracy [the translation] is sound, and it has the higher accuracy of spirit'. Interestingly, the Princess (who is explicitly credited with having translated and edited the English edition of the book) introduced some 'suppressions' which she justified by the 'coarse character of the original'.

The reviewer in the *Saturday Review* continued: '..... Wilhelmine had that fine eighteenth century habit of being outspoken, and has unquestionably spoken of certain matters ....

which a lady of her position, or indeed any lady, in these days would leave among the tacenda'.

The 'outspoken matters' had something to do with Augustus the Strong and Peter the Great, and were obviously potentially too upsetting to the Victorian reader (other than the Princess!). Even the *Literary Churchman* had some nice things to say about the book.

The Princess contributed an interesting eight-page introduction to *The Memoirs,* written at Cumberland Lodge in May 1887. The *Introduction* reveals that she was familiar with the history of the period and had certainly read at least some of Carlyle's *History of Frederick the Great.*

She writes with considerable confidence and her language is strangely modern and unpretentious. Nor was this to be her last encounter with the sister of Frederick the Great of Germany, since she notes that her translation of the correspondence between the Margravine and Voltaire (discovered by Dr. Georg Horn of Berlin in 1865) 'is in preparation'. She writes that '...[Wilhelmine] stands out in marked prominence among the most gifted women of the eighteenth century, not only by her mental powers, but by her goodness of heart, her self-sacrificing devotion, and true friendship'.

In the context, this sounds very much like an early stirring of rudimentary feminism in the breast of a Victorian lady, especially one belonging to the Royal family. And it was all based on some very thorough research carried out in the Royal Library in Berlin.

There is also a remarkable paragraph about the Margravine and her brother whom she describes as 'among the first of those questioning minds that strove after spiritual freedom. They had studied the English philosophers, Newton [sic], Locke, and Shaftesbury, and were roused to enthusiasm by the writings of Voltaire and Rousseau. .... In the eighteenth century began that great struggle of philosophy against tyranny and worn out abuses which culminated in the French Revolution. The noblest minds were engaged in the struggle........'

Could this really be a member of the Royal Family writing *well over a hundred years ago* (even if we recall that the word *struggle* had not yet acquired its modern Marxist connotations)?

Helena's translation of the correspondence between the Margravine and Voltaire appeared in 1888. Voltaire's letters were 'both graceful and witty' and the Princess' translations of them were no mean achievement by any standard. And, of course, it was remarkable that the Princess should have chosen to translate the work of one of the most controversial and original European writers.

There were altogether 25 letters from Voltaire (and the replies from the Margravine). Dr. Horn provided some explanatory notes and it was this collection that Princess Helena translated into English. The translation is crisply idiomatic and was thought by reviewers to give the impression of original writing. The letters cover the period 1742-1758 and '... were believed to be lost. Yet it was but a century's dust which hid them'.

The letters reveal an exchange of ideas and of affection. They contain many quotable expressions which the Princess skilfully reproduced in English. For example, one of Wilhelmine's letters ends with the striking words: '..... think of happiness, renounce repentance, keep well, think sometimes of me, and rely on my perfect esteem'. These were the words of the woman who is described in Helena's translation as '... the magnet which attracted all that was greatest and most celebrated, all that was most worthy of esteem and consideration'.

In addition to these two books Helena wrote a *Memoir* devoted to her sister Alice, the Grand Duchess of Hesse, which was included as an introduction to a collection of Alice's letters. The collection was published by John Murray in 1884 and went through a number of editions[106]. Murray's archives reveal that there was a vigorous discussion as to who held the copyright to these letters and the associated material that had been published in German 1883 by a publisher called Arnold Bergsträsser.

Another translation undertaken by the Princess in 1882, was that of a very popular booklet entitled *First Aid to the Injured,* which was originally published in German by Professor Friedrich Esmarch (the brother in law of Prince Christian and the first person to introduce antisepsis during the Franco-Prussian war). This reflected her interest in nursing. The last edition of this booklet appeared in 1906.

It may well be that during her trips to her sister in Berlin[107] in the 1880s (for example, she was there in 1888), and to the Royal Library there, Helena was in touch with her father's erstwhile librarian. No direct evidence for this survives, but, on the other hand, Ruland's son was asked by his father to destroy his files, which he duly did.[108] And yet, mysteriously, Helena's letters to Carl Ruland do survive. The conclusion may be that Ruland's son saw them as being of transcendent value. It is most unlikely that the emotional Princess had forgotten them – or their author - throughout the years that followed.

The Bergsträsser affair[109]

British royalty has always been regarded as fair game by all kinds of publishers, especially since Queen Victoria effectively adopted the principle that *if you can't beat them, join them*, and thus became a best-selling author herself[110].

And so it was that when a German publisher, Arnold Bergsträsser, published a German translation of the correspondence between Princess Alice (Victoria's second daughter) and her mother, he received a number of lucrative offers from British publishers who hoped to repeat the success of the German book by re-publishing it in English.

The German edition appeared in 1883 and included a biographical sketch of Alice by a Darmstadt clergyman, Dr. Carl Sell, who also introduced the letters and commented in some detail upon them. They were chosen by Sell from a selection made available by the Queen. The situation became somewhat ambiguous, and the associated row very acrimonious, because the Queen subsequently maintained quite firmly that she did not give explicit permission for publication.

Nevertheless, when the German translation of these letters was in fact published in book form, Helena got in touch with Sell and asked for permission to translate his text into English. This he gave without hesitation - and perhaps too hastily - without consulting his German publisher.

Having obtained a copy of the book and having secured Dr. Sell's permission, Helena set about translating the German text (of course, the original letters between Alice and her mother were in English and were available to Helena at Windsor). She may well have been encouraged by her mother's publishing successes and realised that that here was an opportunity for another possible royal best-seller.

However, a totally unexpected difficulty arose in December 1883, by which time her translation was nearing completion. It was a complication of a kind that, because of their elevated status, neither Helena nor the Queen was accustomed to.

On December 8, Helena approached Sir Theodore Martin, her father's biographer and a noted author. 'I am most anxious' she wrote 'to see you and consult with you about a translation I am making of my dear Sister's biography [which has] just come out'.

The reason for her 'anxiety' was that she discovered that Bergsträsser was claiming the ownership of the copyright to the collection of Alice's letters and, on this basis, demanded a delay in the publication of the English-language edition.

In response to her request, Martin met Helena in the home of a friend, Admiral Sir Frederick Nicolson, near Albert Gate in London, and was invited by Helena to act informally as an intermediary between her and Bergsträsser. He was authorised to conclude an agreement that would clear the way for the publication of Alice's letters together with Sell's text in English. At more or less the same time, Helena also asked the royal librarian Hermann Sahl, who had connections in Darmstadt, to act as another intermediary

These exchanges eventually elicited a reply from Bergsträsser in the form of a letter to Martin on December 29. 'I have been informed by Mr. Sahl', he wrote to Sir Theodore, 'that Princess Christian wishes to regulate the matter of the book .... through your esteemed self.'. He went on to point out that he had had 'numerous offers' from English publishers and that the eventual publisher of the English-language edition could expect a 'high honorarium'. And he concluded with a request for a personal interview with Martin for which he was willing to travel to London.

However, before that interview took place, Bergsträsser was persuaded to abandon his attempts to delay the publication of the English edition and to modify his copyright claim in return for a suitable sum of money. Meanwhile, Helena wrote to Martin: 'I am working as hard as I can, but the translation is not easy ..... the German is so flowery and the sentences endless'. She also needed some help from Martin with the formulation of the Preface.

Bergsträsser finally came to London in January to meet Martin face to face and to agree royalty terms, but Helena was insisting on behalf of the Queen that the copyright in the letters was actually irrevocably the Queen's and that only Sell's text was open to negotiation. In fact, both royal ladies regarded Bergsträsser's demands as unjustified if not impertinent.

Having met Martin, Bergsträsser finally agreed in a letter of January 12 to accept £100 for the first three thousand copies and a further £40 pounds for each subsequent thousand copies sold. Unfortunately, he seemed throughout to regard all these agreements as inconclusive and continued to argue about the sums allegedly due to him whilst the royals regarded him as a troublesome gadfly, and would not communicate with him directly.

What Bergsträsser did not reckon with was that at the end of these negotiations he had to deal not with the relatively amateurish efforts of Martin and Sahl, but with the hard-headed publisher in the shape of John Murray who was finally chosen as the English publisher of Alice's letters. The other candidates - Macmillan and Sampson Low, Marston and Co. - had their applications dismissed by Martin very early on, despite the fact that the Queen favoured Macmillan.

Murray insisted[111] on seeing the original publication contracts (if any) in Bergsträsser's possession and also a copy of the informal agreement with Martin (which no-one else had seen[112]). It is not clear whether he was allowed sight of any of these documents, but he must have been paid off more or less in line with the original proposal engineered by Martin, although, in Helena's words, Bergsträsser 'no doubt will receive far more than he is really at all entitled to'. This really seemed to trouble her, as witnessed by her numerous letters to Martin and Murray between December and July of 1884. There is little doubt that the Queen and her daughter assumed that they would get their own way and seemed startled when they were confronted by someone unwilling to submit to their wishes..

In the event, the first English edition sold out almost immediately, but for the second edition, published in 1885, Murray introduced his final master stroke. He removed Sell's biographical introduction and replaced it with a substantial 53-page *Memoir* commissioned from Princess Christian herself, having warned the Princess to avoid 'the appearance of too great coincidence with Sell's text being commented upon'. He also added some extracts from the Queen's *Journal* and a brief concluding piece by Sir Theodore Martin.

All this had two obvious advantages: first, a royalty was no longer due on Sell's introduction and, second, extra publicity was attracted by the fact that Princess Christian's name appeared on the title page as the author of the new *Memoir*.

The review in *The Times* described the *Memoir* as 'a touching biographical sketch, written by the Princess Christian, containing not only unpublished extracts from Her Majesty's private journals, but the sad story of the death-bed scenes at Darmstadt, described by a devoted friend of the Grand Duchess who attended her in her last illness..... This loving little memoir by the Princess Christian gives us a higher and clearer insight into the beautiful character of one of the most estimable and lovable of women'.

This - and other similar reviews elsewhere - simply ensured that the book continued to sell in substantial numbers (the print run for the Alice letters was 20,000 copies) and, together with the three books she translated, provided Helena with some useful additional income. The collection of Alice's letters was still available twelve years later. The appetite of the reading public for royal books was unsatiable.

Beautiful, talented and helpful

There are other sources in which Princess Helena is discussed in much more sympathetic terms than those found in the letters and memoirs of her mother and some members of the circle closely centred on Queen Victoria.

In 1956, Helena's daughter Marie Louise published a striking (and best-selling) book of reminiscences[113] in which she presented a picture that was rather different from that found elsewhere. Here Helena is described as 'very lovely, with wavy brown hair, a beautiful little straight nose, and lovely amber-coloured eyes....... She was very talented: played the piano exquisitely, had a distinct gift for drawing and painting in water-colours..... Her outstanding gift was loyalty to her friends........ She was brilliantly clever, had a wonderful head for business.......'.

Strangely, Princes Marie Louise makes no detailed reference in her memoirs, written in the 1950s, to her mother's writing which attracted so much favourable comment. Marie Louise herself seems to have inherited her mother's writing talent: she published two other works[114] in addition to her very successful *Memories* that rapidly went into a second edition.

In her childhood and in her teenage years, Helena showed considerable talent for drawing. Augusta Stanley marvelled at the drawings Helena produced at the age of only three[115]. At eleven, Helena's precocity at draughtsmanship reached remarkable levels.

Lady Knightley, Helena's close friend, describes her in her *Journals* in 1882 as 'rayonnante de jeunesse et d'intelligence'. Earlier, in 1863, she writes about her as 'looking very handsome.........and very much admired by all the foreigners at Windsor'. Again, in 1868 she records in her *Journals* that 'Princess Christian looked so nice, and it is a pleasure to watch her constantly changing expression'. And two years earlier, in November 1866, not long after her wedding, Benjamin Disraeli described[116] her as 'very good looking, & vivacious'.

Helena was, as one might say today, a very determined *problem solver*. Because of her Royal status she was often able to help others with domestic or medical problems. It was not unknown for her to motor up to London to tackle some senior official - especially in the War Office (where she had friends) - on behalf of an aggrieved family in Windsor. She had a predilection for direct speaking. Typically, in the course of a major dock strike, she once observed that 'prayers do not settle strikes'!

The Princess frequently took on the role of a kind of mothers' ombudsman. For example, she was in touch with Colonel Mends of the King's Royal Rifles because this was the regiment that her son served with. On February 22, 1900, she wrote to Mends asking for assistance in finding a Private Thomson[117] a 20-year old soldier missing in the South African war. 'I feel so sorry for these poor mothers who do not know what has become of their sons' - she wrote from Cumberland Lodge.

She obviously knew how to exploit her position for the good of others. Indeed, because of her Royal status, she must have had a reply by return of post because three days later Colonel Mends received a postcard thanking him for his help. And by March 25, Private Thomson was found in Pretoria with the further help of the American Ambassador whom the Princess also approached. Of course, she did not know that later that year she was to mourn her own son, Christian Victor, who died in South Africa in October 1900 at the age of only 33.

St. Martin's place

On July 19, 1870 Napoleon III was provoked into declaring war on Prussia, but was decisively beaten (and indeed captured on September 2 at Sedan) by Bismarck's forces. On January 28, 1871 France was forced to sign an armistice.

The war was not only a humiliation for France, but it was also costly in lost lives, in lost territory and in the payment to the Prussians of what was effectively a huge fine.

Britain was not directly involved in 'Bismarck's three wars' (Schleswig-Holstein in 1864, Austro-Prussian in 1866 and Franco-German in 1870), but the Queen and her family inevitably were. After all, her eldest daughter Victoria was married to the Prussian Crown Prince who eventually became the German Emperor Frederick III and, before he reached that elevated position, commanded the troops that fought the Austrians much against his better judgement. Another daughter, Princess Alice, was married to Louis IV, Grand Duke of Hesse-Darmstadt, and her brother in law was Ernest II Duke of Saxe-Coburg-Gotha. It is therefore not difficult to guess which side attracted the sympathy of most of the British fraction of the Saxe-Coburg mafia. This was a difficulty for both the British foreign policy makers and for the Queen, all of whom were united in their desire to keep out of the conflict.

But sympathy was not enough and it was to the obvious credit of the 24-year old Princess Christian that she soon found a practical way of helping the victims of war - on both sides.

The Franco-Prussian war was a particularly nasty one. Thousands upon thousands of soldiers marched across Europe to engage in direct conflict in which there were huge casualties on both sides.

Within three days of the declaration of war, the course of which was reported in great detail in the British press, a letter (dated July 22) was published in *The Times* by Colonel Robert Loyd-Lindsay V.C. who had distinguished himself in the Crimean War in which he witnessed the great suffering of soldiers and was subsequently Gentleman-in-Waiting to the Prince of Wales[118]. He wrote:

> 'The news which daily reaches us from abroad shows that nations can at times go mad as well as individuals. It is strange to read in your columns of the preparations which are being made simultaneously to destroy life and to save it. Unfortunately, it is far easier to destroy than to save, all the glory being reserved for the former, and ten times the amount of scientific resources being devoted to it. .... there will be large amount of sympathy excited on behalf of the wounded soldiers on both sides - for the French, our staunch and faithful allies in the Crimea .... for the Prussians, related to us by ties of friendship and by our Princess Royal destined to be their Queen. '

He went on to draw attention to the existence of the *Society for Aiding and Ameliorating the Condition of the Sick and Wounded of Armies in Time of War*. This derived from an idea of a Swiss businessman Henry Dunant who, having witnessed the appalling suffering of soldiers wounded in the battle of Solferino, suggested the formation of an international movement for the relief of such suffering in wartime, based on some international principle acceptable to all nations.

As a direct result of this, a conference of 16 states, including Great Britain, was convened in Geneva in 1863 and, on August 22, 1864, twelve states signed the Geneva Convention. Great Britain was among the remaining four who delayed joining. However, all sixteen states ratified or acceded to the Convention by 1867 and the United States joined in 1882. This was the beginning of the *International Red Cross* movement, the red cross on a white background being adopted as the emblem of it.

Although by mid-1860s there were over thirty Red Cross societies in Europe, and although the British Government formally supported the convention and indeed sent a delegate to the original meeting, no such society was established in England until Colonel Loyd-Lindsay called, in *The Times,* for the formation of a Committee similar to the many such committees already functioning on the continent of Europe. As a token of the importance he attached to this, he deposited £1,000 at Coutts Bank (with which his family was associated) to the account of the *Society for Aid to the Sick and Wounded in War.*

Princess Christian: a cartoon published in ***London Figaro*** *in* 1874

Soon after, on August 4, a public meeting was held in London and the *National Society for Aid to the Sick and Wounded in War* was formed and adopted the rules of the Geneva Convention of 1864. This was the beginning of a national Red Cross movement in Great Britain.

Robert Loyd-Lindsay had been supported in this venture by Professor Thomas Longmore of the Royal Victoria Hospital who was the British delegate to the original conference in Geneva, sent there by the War Office, and by John (later Sir John) Furley. A committee of twenty two members was established with Loyd-Lindsay as chairman, Queen Victoria as Patron and the Prince of Wales (later Edward VII) as President.

Princess Christian became Chairman of the Ladies' Committee of the Society, and there was also a Ladies' Working Committee in London with Mrs. Harriet Loyd-Lindsay, the wife of the Colonel, playing a leading part[119].

The Ladies' Working Committee at first operated from 2 St. Martin's Place. This was part of a complex of old premises adjacent to the St. Martin's Workhouse, which were eventually demolished in the late 1880s (the National Portrait Gallery was built on the land thus made available). Rate books for 1870 and 1871 suggest that the premises of the Society were provided by the Office of Works[120]. After a while, they became too small and the Government provided two further houses across the road. 'We have annexed a whole wing of the St. Martin's disused Workhouse' - wrote Mrs. Loyd-Lindsay to her mother[121] - 'a gloomy suite of rooms, dirty and dusty but roomy. Large, however, as they are, they are not sufficient for the hundreds of bales which keep pouring in. ..... I remembered to have heard that there were large vaults under St. Martin's Churchyard, so I sallied forth, roused up the head church warden, and persuaded him to give us the use of the vaults. ... The vaults are ..... filled with long lines of beautifully packed bales ... really a noble sight'. This great expansion was a consequence of the tremendous response elicited in England by the correspondence in *The Times* and by reports elsewhere in the press.

Whilst six packers were hard at work all day, there were several men and women who unpacked and sorted all the parcels that were flooding in. Princess Christian at the head of a team of several well-known ladies spent a great deal of time there, writing to people who were thought to be suitable targets for appeals and dealing with all matters in which her prestige as the Sovereign's daughter could be - and was - helpful.

Surviving correspondence between Princess Christian and Harriet Loyd-Lindsay[122], who together with her husband was very active in the running of the society, shows that the Princess' contribution was not at all merely cosmetic. She was not just a 'name' employed to attract people's attention. Indeed, she had clear talent for befriending, guiding and encouraging the people working with her and for her. She could be quite affectionate towards ladies she liked and trusted, but she was always firm on matters of principle or policy, especially whenever there was anything that could impinge on public policy. This was very remarkable for a lady of only twenty four.

There was never the remotest hint of snobbery or uppishness or any doubt about her dedication to the cause.

Only two days after the formation of the National Committee, Princess Christian was firing off letters to friends and 'collecting lint and bandages'. In a string of almost daily letters to Mrs. Lindsay, she reported that she was collecting material and, for example, that a Mr. Balfour ('whom I met the other day and who heard us speak of the Society') had sent her a cheque for £1,000. This young man was to become the Prime Minister of Great Britain in 1902.

The fund-raising was so successful that, by the end of March 1871, nearly £300,000 had been collected. As a sign of neutrality, the Committee instructed Loyd-Lindsay to give £40,000 in cash to both sides. He delivered this gift of money in person. Unfortunately for the French, the Prussians were still on French territory (at Versailles) to receive it.

The National Committee also provided surgeons, nurses, administrative support, ambulances and many other things. Princess Christian was involved directly in all these matters, including personal interviewing of nurses before they were sent abroad.

It was not until 1898 that it was decided after consultation with the War Office to establish a Central Red Cross Committee for the British Empire and its Dependencies. This again included Princess Christian, representing the Army Nursing Service which was created in 1897 under her presidency. She thus had a foot in both the voluntary and government sectors. And for her work during the Franco-German war she was awarded the Bronze Cross of the

French Red Cross Society (among 48 other members of the National Society).

Of course, as usual, the development of an organisation - even voluntary organisation - gave rise to discussions of infrastructure costs. On this the Princess was very clear. 'The Council [of the Central British Red Cross]' - she wrote from Cumberland Lodge a few years later - 'has never had the slightest wish or intention of creating any extensive or expensive system of highly paid officials and officers. All the Council think necessary is one central office, thoroughly organised, and one secretary conversant with the duties to carry on the important work of the office. The Council desire nothing more than the most simple organisation'[123] . Here, then, was the anti-bureaucratic principle at work.

There was also some discussion of a possible conflict of responsibility or even intention between the War Office and the Red Cross. The Princess seemed to think that there was no real controversy about this in the case of a 'big war', since the War Office would have to rely on the help of Voluntary Aid Societies because 'the burden of keeping up in time of peace a medical organisation sufficient to cope with the requirements of a big war would be intolerable'.

She then concluded her letter to Mrs. Lloyd-Lindsay with the words: 'I think you will now see that what our Council wants is nothing more than what you approve of'. There was a certain line that could not be overstepped. Indeed, here was a glimpse of the hard fact that beneath the polite Victorian phraseology there was a firm definition of who was really who.

The public profile of the Princess continued to evolve in the course of all these events. By 1874, *The London Figaro* could no longer resist the temptation of flattering both its readers and the Princess. Its editor and proprietor, one James Mortimer, produced the following piece in the issue of the magazine of December 23, 1874: 'The third daughter of the Queen has for eight years been married to Prince 102, . There is no lady in the land who is more courted by society or more affectionately regarded by friends. A party at which she is present is sure to be a great success. Following the example of her mother, the princess not only gives money to the poor, but takes an active personal interest in the book of charity.' And he pushed it even harder by underlining a cartoon of the Princess with a quotation from Milton's *Paradise Lost:*

> *Grace was in all her steps - heaven in her eye*
> *In every gesture dignity and love.*

Over 120 years later, it is hard to say what all this really meant or whether it was - at least partly - as embarrassing as it looks now. Or perhaps it was the Victorian equivalent of modern tabloid babble that was merely the expected background noise issuing from printed pages?

There must have been some real public interest in such matters because the magazine proclaimed near its masthead that '..... the present number of *The London Figaro* is accompanied by an elegant chronograph of HRH Pss. Helena. Every newsvendor is bound to deliver the chronograph supplement to purchasers of this paper, without extra charge'. At the same time the price of *The London Figaro* was reduced from 2d to 1d! Royalty was - as it is now - a topic that helped to sell newspapers and magazines.

The Princess continued to work for the Red Cross after the end the Franco-German war. In the last thirty years of the nineteenth century there were seven major conflicts in which the Red Cross offered significant contribution. But there were difficulties with the proliferation of organisations, conflicting personal interests and organisational obstacles. They were finally overcome in 1905 when The British Red Cross Society was formed at the insistence of Edward VII, with the King as Patron and Queen Alexandra as President. The formal direction and control at the very top was thus assured, but hard practical work by prestigious people such Princess Christian remained an unavoidable necessity.

No. 2 St. Martin's Lane is today the address of the National Portrait Gallery which is the depository of the photographs and paintings of famous people, including those of Princess Christian and her family.

South Africa

A shipping station was established at the Cape of Good Hope by the Dutch East India Company in 1652. The early settlers were Dutch farmers who eventually referred to themselves as Afrikaners and spoke a language called Afrikaans. From the Cape they expanded their activities deeper into Southern Africa, and those of them who undertook to *trekken* (i.e., to *travel* in Middle Dutch) into the African interior were the *trekboers.*

This was the origin of the verb *to trek* and the noun *Boer,* which eventually became part of the English language.

In the nineteenth century, there were three factors that dominated the affairs of Southern Africa. First, the Cape became a naval base on the route to India and the East. For obvious strategic reasons, Britain took over the Cape Colony in 1806 as its permanent possession, with the Boers as the majority of the whites.

In 1843 Britain added Natal to its list of directly controlled territories, and in 1852 and 1854 she recognised Transvaal and the Orange Free State as independent Boer republics.

Towards the end of the nineteenth century, the discovery of diamond and gold deposits led to the diamond rush of 1870 and the gold rush of 1886. These deposits eventually became the source of great wealth both for the territory as a whole and for certain powerful people individually. However, the situation was changed again by Britain's annexation of Transvaal in 1877, which led directly three years later, in 1880, to a Boer revolt led by Paul Kruger. The result was a serious reverse for the British army in the region, ending with its defeat in the Battle of Manjuba Hill. Republican self-government under Paul Kruger was restored to Transvaal by the Gladstone government in 1884 and Britain retained only control over Transvaal's foreign affairs.

Demographically, the situation was unstable. At first, few Britons were tempted to emigrate to Southern Africa, but diamonds and gold eventually proved too much of an attraction and the Uitlanders, the new, mostly British, immigrants, began to outnumber the Boers in the Transvaal without acquiring the corresponding political rights because of voting restrictions imposed by the Boer-dominated administration.

Uitlander dissatisfaction with their political status, and perceived physical discrimination, eventually led in December 1895 to the so-called Jameson Raid whereby a certain Dr. Leander Starr Jameson, encouraged by British interests, led a force of only a few hundred men into the Boer republic of Transvaal in the hope of amplifying his efforts by means of local support. This support did not materialise and the raid failed totally. Dr. Jameson was arrested and Cecil Rhodes who played a covert role in the affair was revealed as the man behind Jameson and had to resign as prime minister of Cape Colony.

It so happened that Princess Christian was at dinner[124] given by Lord Salisbury at Hatfield House on January 3, 1896 when an urgent 'red box' arrived. The Prime Minister asked the Princess for permission to open it and found it contained a single sheet of paper. It informed the Prime Minister that the Kaiser attempted to interfere in the aftermath of the Jameson Raid by sending an open telegram to Kruger, congratulating him on his success in defending his country against 'attack from without'. The Kaiser had a number of reasons for this intervention: one of them was that Germany had substantial investment in the Traansval; another was that he enjoyed twisting the tail of the British lion.

Salisbury read the message, annotated it and sent it back to the Foreign Office. When the Princess asked 'What answer have you sent?', Salisbury is said to have replied: 'I have sent no answer. I sent ships'. There are other versions of this anecdote, but they are less amusing and not significantly different in their content In fact, the Kaiser's telegram fairly quickly disappeared into the historical undergrowth.

The appointment of Alfred Milner in 1897 as High Commissioner for Southern Africa in the wake of the Jameson fiasco made things even worse. Milner was dedicated to a single ideal, namely, the pursuance by all possible means of British imperial interests in Southern Africa. Kruger took the opposite line: he saw his task as the defence of Boer independence in the face of British imperial and economic ambitions as well as internal pressures by numerous enterprising and successful Uitlanders who paid taxes, but did not have proportionate political rights. And in distant London, Colonial Secretary Joseph Chamberlain tried to cool the situation by diplomatic moves that were often misunderstood by Kruger and undermined by Milner. This human triangle inevitably led to war (probably wished for by Milner as a means of acquiring the entire area for the British Empire).

Threats explicit and implied continued to be exchanged between the British and the Boers, with the former strengthening their military positions. In October 1899 President Kruger issued an ultimatum in which he demanded with support of the Orange Free State that Britain should withdraw its forces on his borders and stop other troops en route to Southern Africa. Almost by definition, an ultimatum such as this could not be accepted or even believed by an imperial power of the size that Kruger was threatening, and so the war inevitably followed.

The Boer forces moved into Natal and Northern Cape and laid siege to Ladysmith (four months), Kimberley (four months) and Mafeking (six months). They imposed major defeats on the British army, culminating in the victory in the battle of Spion Kop in January 1890. This was the end of the painful lesson given to the

British by the Boers. Thereafter, reinforcements led by Lords Roberts and Kitchener eventually relieved the besieged towns and began the fight back in the face of guerrilla tactics by the Boers. The British forces responded to these tactics by rounding up the families of the guerrillas and placing them in concentration camps as well as pursuing a scorched earth policy of Boer farm burning as a major component. Another tactic was to create protected areas using lines of barbed wire fences guarded at regular intervals by earth and iron blockhouses. There were thousands of these blockhouses with 66,000 troops looking after them[125].

Whilst these measures eventually brought the war to an end with the signing of the Peace of Vereening on May 31, 1902, the methods adopted by the British generals attracted considerable criticism in Britain and on the continent of Europe. However, the result achieved at great cost was really predictable: the British Empire reasserted itself in Southern Africa. Transvaal and Orange free State were annexed permanently, and English became the official language, but Dutch was allowed in schools and courts, and the Boers were offered some financial assistance

The facts emerging in the aftermath of the war were shocking. More than six thousand British soldiers were killed in the field and sixteen thousand more died from enteric fever. The total number of soldiers engaged on the British side was approximately 350,000 and the total number on the Boer side was about 90,000 (7,000 deaths).

The number of civilian deaths in the concentration camps was of the order of 25,000. No-one knows how many black Africans died during the war. They must have run into thousands.

As in the 1870s in Europe, Princess Helena now began a new project to help British soldiers wounded in the Boer war. She persuaded the Central British Red Cross Committee to provide a sum of money for the building and equipping of a complete hospital train of seven bogie carriages. The contract for this train was signed in October 1899 with the Birmingham Carriage and Wagon Company. The project was completed in December of that year and the Princess went to Birmingham to inspect the train and some of the stores, which included gifts from the Queen, the Princess herself and members of the Royal Family. The Borough of Windsor contributed £6,100 to the cost and the Princess added £650 from some funds invested in her name.

The seven-carriage train was named *The Princess Christian Hospital Train.* It was reassembled in Durban in February 1900 and was used extensively in South Africa to transport over 7,500 wounded soldiers. The train was lavishly equipped and highly spoken of by everyone who worked in it. It was the first train to enter Ladysmith after it was relieved.[126]

Similar Princess Christian Trains were used in World War I in Europe[127] and in the Chanak Affair in Turkey in 1922. In the latter case, British troops were sent to Constantinople and other towns on the Dardanelles in the aftermath of World War I. A train loaded with stores for the refugees from the conflict incorporated four ambulance coaches loaned by Princess Helena. The train used in Europe cost £25,000 and was funded by the Princess[128].

In the ghastly Boer war, one of the Lord Roberts' ADCs was Prince Christian Victor, Princess Helena's first son. He was educated at Wellington College and at Magdalen College, Oxford. At Wellington he played for the college First Eleven in 1883 and was captain of the cricket team in 1885. After Sandhurst (where he was also captain of cricket), he was commissioned in the 60th King's Royal Rifles in 1888. He reached the rank of captain in 1896 and Brevet Major later in that year.

Christian Victor did not have a distinguished academic career, but was an able cricketer. In his own words, '.... I always had a more intimate acquaintance with *square leg* than *square root*'[129]. His arrival in South Africa followed his service in the Ashanti campaign in 1895-86 and in the battles of Atbara and Khartoum. Like many others, he died of enteric fever in the Yeomanry Hospital in Pretoria on October 29, 1900 after a fortnight's illness[130]. He was buried in the Pretoria cemetery on November 1, 1900. The grave is marked by a granite cross and a cast iron railing.

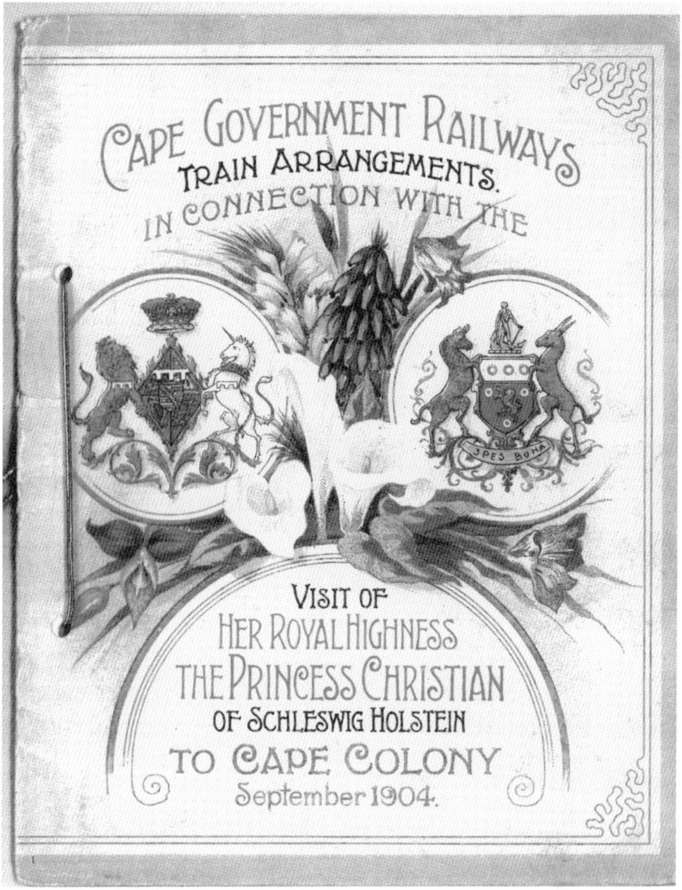

The death of Prince Christian Victor was a severe shock to his family. Eventually, Helena decided that a way of dealing with the loss of her son was to go to South Africa to visit her son's grave. Accordingly, on August 20, 1904 she sailed from Southampton in the *Wilmer Castle*, accompanied by her daughter Victoria ('Thora'). They docked in Table Bay on September 6.

The visit was ostensibly a private one, but no-one could really imagine that the visit to South Africa after a bitter war between the Boer republics and Britain by someone who was not only a daughter of Queen Victoria, but also a sister of the reigning king - Edward VII - would in the end be anything but private.

Two years after the signing of the peace agreement, Southern Africa was entirely under British control and so the Princess was able to spend a month visiting all parts of the country, covering a total of 4,000 miles. She travelled via Kimberley, Mafeking and Bulawayo to Victoria Falls where an island was later named after her. On the way back she visited Johannesburg and Pretoria, eventually reaching the Cape via Pietermaritzburg, Durban and Bloemfontain.

Wherever she went she was treated as an ambassador for Britain. The authorities provided the appropriate ceremonial and she laid foundation stones and attended receptions, garden parties, bazaars and so on. She opened the Princess Christian Park and the Princess Christian Home for elderly ladies. She made particular point of meeting both Boers and Britons, and her visit gradually emerged as a significant contribution to reconciliation after a bitter war. She had a successful meeting with Boer General Louis Botha, but General Jan Smuts refused to meet her, probably because one of his children died in a British concentration camp (many years later he expressed his regret for this snub).

On Friday, September 23, the Princess visited her son's grave in Pretoria. By then, she was aware of a somewhat mysterious sequence of events that was briefly mentioned in both British and South African press.

On two occasions just prior to the arrival of the Princess in South Africa, two attempts were made by persons unknown to remove Prince Christian Victors body from its grave in Pretoria. On one of these occasions, the covering slab was reported by Reuters to have been 'broken'. The Mayor hastily obtained the necessary funds to clear up the mess. Public indignation then led the Transvaal Government to offer a reward of £200 for the apprehension of the desecrators of Christian Victor's grave. In fact, no-one was apprehended, but two guesses were offered as to the reason for the attempt to remove the Prince's body: either the perpetrators of the outrage were after some kind of a ransom or there was a political motive behind the attempt by a Boer faction wishing to embarrass the British authorities. There was no firm evidence for either suggestion.

On her farewell visit to her son's grave, the Princess presented a signed photograph to the florist who always attended to the grave. She thanked his children who were in the habit of placing flowers on the grave and personally asked them to continue the custom. She entered a reminder in their birthday books and promised to revisit the grave.

A month after her arrival, the Princess sailed home on the Kildonan Castle, having travelled several thousand miles in the consolidated British possessions in Southern Africa. By then, she had acquired a legion of admirers. This was Royalty at its best.

Mrs. Williams' school

Chevalier de Seingalt, born on April 2, 1725 in Venice, now belongs to the exlusive group of people whose surnames have become common nouns in the English language. Indeed, a man known for his amorous adventures is commonly referred to as a *Casanova*, the true name of the talented and charming adventurer who paraded under the assumed name of Chevalier de Seingalt. His travels took him to European capitals - ranging from London to St. Petersburg - in which many found the force of his talented personality totally irresistible, as witnessed by the 12 volumes of his splendid memoirs.

In May 1753 he met in Venice a lady of considerable talent (and not only talent) who was to acquire an almost comparably exotic history.

She was Madame Theresa Pompeati, later usually known in London as Mrs. Cornelys, erstwhile wife of a well known dancer (Angelo Pompeati, who committed suicide just before her departure to Italy). She had been an opera singer in Amsterdam and in London, the mistress of some famous men, including the Margrave of Bayreuth. She later became the proprietor of the notorious and palatial Carlisle House on the east side of Soho Square in London, which she purchased in about 1759. It was about her that Casanova said in his memoirs[131] '*She was an excellent musician, but her fortune was not altogether owing to her talent; her charms had done more for her than anything else'.*

Mrs. Cornelys clearly dominated the world of fashion and entertainment in the 1760s with her lavish presentations in huge rooms luxuriously fitted out in Carlisle House. With music, food and possibly other entertainments and facilities also provided, this was a venue that people who could afford it could not resist, especially when faced by Mrs. Cornelys' tempting advertising in London newspapers.

Mrs. Cornelys' talents in showmanship and publicity were matched by her ability to establish connections with nobility and - however remotely- with royalty too. A plaque discovered after Carlisle House was eventually sold and demolished to make way for the present-day St. Patrick's Church carried the following description:

Not Vain but Grateful
In Honour of the Society
And my First Protectress Ye
HON^BLE^ M^RS.^ ELIZABETH CHUDLEIGH
Is Laid the First Stone
Of this Edifice June 19, 1761
by me TERESA CORNELYS

The Mrs. Chudleigh in question was in fact a maid to the Prince of Wales who married a nobleman and, as it turned out, was eventually exiled for bigamy. This combination of indirect channels to the highest places in the land and a somewhat suspect personality somewhere along the link was not an untypical of Mrs. Cornelys.

However, after several years of extravagant success in Soho Square, where her numerous and phenomenally lavish balls and masquerades were patronised in large numbers by royalty, nobility, gentry and (separately) wealthy commoners, her expenditure exceeded her income and in 1771 she was in serious debt, facing bailiffs. In 1771 she was fined by Bow Street Magistrates for keeping a disorderly house. Bankruptcy followed and, after some further unsuccessful attempts to recover her balance, Mrs. Cornelys found herself in debtors' prison. She died in Fleet Prison in 1797, still holding on to 'visionary prospects' which she would not resign, and, 'while she was dreaming of a palace, she died in gaol'[132].

The conjunction of these two extraordinary characters - Casanova and Pompeati - produced in 1753 in Venice a daughter - Sophie Wilhelmina - who under the assumed name of Mrs. Williams eventually became, in 1820, the Honorary Secretary and Sub-Treasurer of the *Adult Orphan Institution* in London. The Institution was formed on June 24, 1820 under the patronage of Princess Augusta, the second daughter (among the 15 children) of George III and Queen Charlotte.

The antecedents of Mrs. Williams were recently explored by Donald Clarke and are described in his remarkable book entitled *A Daisy in a Broom.*

Sophie's education in a well-known Hammersmith boarding school in London, with fees said to be paid at least in part by Casanova, led to contacts with aristocratic families who admired her striking musical talents and her fluent knowledge of foreign languages (French and Italian), which equipped her for positions with wealthy families in London. And, like her mother (whose English, by the way, was initially poor and subsequently never perfect), she had a very useful ability to attach herself to significant society figures. She eventually became a Private Almoner to Princess Augusta and, in 1820, the effective manager of one of Augusta's favourite projects, namely, the Adult Orphan Institution, which in a reincarnated form is now a school called the *Princess Helena College.*

The idea of an *Adult Orphan Institution* was first mooted by Mrs. Williams with Queen Charlotte, the wife of George III. Queen Charlotte approved, which naturally resulted in a considerable list of notable supporters of the idea of an 'Asylum for those Orphan Daughters of the Clergy, and of Military and Naval Officers, who should be left friendless or unprovided to contend with the hardship and temptations of to which they might be exposed'.

And so on June 24, 1820, the Institution was indeed formed with Princess Augusta as its sole patron and Mrs. Williams as its 'Honorary Secretary and Sub-Treasurer'. The Institution began its existence at 32-33 Mornington Place in North London and for the next three years Mrs. Williams succeeded in putting it on its feet with the support of the King and of the Nobility of the time. The Institution was ran by a Gentlemen's Committee and a somewhat less authoritative Ladies' Committee.

Mrs. Williams died on June 25, 1823 and in 1824 the Institution moved to a permanent home designed by Nash and located in Regent's Park, at 11 St. Andrew's Place, on a piece of land donated by the Crown at £100 per annum. The final cost, including furniture, was £6,000 - £7,000.

Mrs. Williams became in the course of time a somewhat mysterious figure. A contemporary account of her personal history before she created the Institution is given in a book by John Taylor[133]. Whilst Mrs. Williams is described in glowing terms by Princess Augusta in the records of the Institution, John Taylor is very much less complimentary about her earlier conduct, though no-one doubted her considerable talents or her ability to get on with many notable social figures of the time. Indeed the generosity of her aristocratic friends provided her with permanent annual income sufficient to keep her in good comfort even without further monies that must have come her way in the service of Princess Augusta.

The identification of Mrs. Williams as the daughter of Teresa Cornelys seems convincing, though it is tempting to speculate that further research may throw additional light on this interesting lady who looks innocent enough playing the harp in the only surviving portrait of her (at the Helena College).

One point that does not seem to have been spotted before is that the names Sophie Wilhelmine given by Mrs. Cornelys to her daughter were also the forenames of the Margravine of Bayreuth, and it is possible that Mrs. Cornelys was influenced in this choice by her intimate relationship with the Margrave.

Moreover we know that in the 1880s, Princess Christian translated the biography of the Margravine. Is it too fanciful to speculate that the Princess may have come across the connection between Mrs. Williams and Mrs. Cornelys after she became associated with the Institution, and that this led her to her interest in the Margravine? At any event, she would have become aware in the course of her translation of the Margravine's *Memoirs* that the Margrave had a number of liaisons whilst married to Wilhelmine. And Helena carried out detailed research in the 1880s in the Royal Library in Berlin, whilst her own large library at Cumberland Lodge may well have contained a copy of John Taylor's book.

Princess Christian became a patron of the Institution in 1868, the President of the Ladies' Committee in 1874 and President overall in 1879. These posts were no mere sinecures for her. Mrs. Williams ensured that the Institution survived its infancy and Princess Helena saw to it that it emerged successfully from its adolescence and early middle age.

In today's terminology, Helena was an excellent manager and very businesslike. She expected agendas and minutes of meetings to be available and was very successful in her attempts to preserve the physical infrastructure of the school. Redecoration and provision of equipment and furniture were well looked after. Her royal status placed considerable authority behind all her requests for action, and when she assumed the post of President overall, the name of the Institution was changed to *The Princess Helena College for Young Ladies* (for boarders) and *High School for Girls* (day juniors) although the latter title was eventually abandoned.

Interestingly, Helena had on her council (which eventually, and at her suggestion, consisted of both ladies and gentlemen) some friends from other times, including the famous singer Jenny Lind who stayed with her at Cumberland Lodge and Harriet Lloyd Lindsay (later Lady Wantage) who worked with her so well at St. Martin's Place. Prince Christian was also a member and attended many of the meetings.

One interesting alumnus of the Institution was Sarah Anne Hildyard who had been appointed in 1847 as Governess to the children of Queen Victoria under Lady Lyttleton, and continued in that post until 1864. She was then elected to the Ladies' Committee on which she continued to serve for another fifteen years.

The College eventually moved to Eaton Rise in Ealing (1882) and to its final location in Preston near Hitchin in Hertfortshire (in

1935) where it continues today. But in the crucial period between 1878 and 1882, Princess Helena was busy 'standing the school on its feet. She presided over seventy of the meetings of the school's council. .... She functioned in effect as her own Chairman of the Governing Council and Committee and in some ways also as her own, long-range, Headmistress-Bursar, with a Lady Superintendent on the spot, as her Right-Hand Woman' .

The Princess was probably responsible for rescuing the school from total oblivion, both by helping with funding campaigns and by her hands-on approach to school management. She almost always supported moves towards the liberalisation of the school regime. As her daughter Marie Louise wrote many years later 'she had a wonderful head for business' .

Naturally enough, new generations are often critical of their elders, and while Helena admired 'her girls', one of them observed much later that she was 'a dowdy, dumpy old lady - like an imitation of Queen Victoria'.

Others saw her very differently, even when she was indeed an old lady. She was described as 'somewhat stout and of dignified bearing, holding her head well thrown back; ...... her face rather pale, her eyes bright blue, with a keen sense of humour lurking therein and showing itself also in the corners of her firm mouth'. She had a 'slightly foreign intonation [that was] not unpleasant[134].

Nursing [135]

The British Nurses' Association (with its very correct apostrophe in the title) was formed in 1887 and Princess Christian was, because of her extensive interests in nursing, a natural candidate for its presidency. She was duly appointed to the post when RBNA was formally launched in 1888. The prefix 'Royal' was added to the title in 1891 and the Royal Charter was granted to the Association in the following year. The Princess was very serious and very practical about the Association; she even designed its badge and incorporated in it her father's motto (*Steadfast and True*)[136].

At the time, the nursing community was racked by internal conflicts that resulted in a number of campaigns for and against the *state registration* of nurses. Antagonisms arising from differences between firmly held beliefs and between strong, and sometimes strong-headed, personalities were involved. But the Princess saw very clearly that there were two preconditions for the advancement of nursing.

First, there was training. In a letter to *The Times* on July 19, 1888, she emphasised that for the training of nurses to be effectual, 'it must be of considerable duration and embrace a variety of experience, and must be guided by careful and systematic teaching'. Second, the Princess saw her function as president of the Association as working towards 'improving the education and *status* of those devoted and self-sacrificing women whose whole lives have been devoted to tending the sick, the suffering, and the dying'. In this - her own - statement made in June 1893 there lurks the italicised word *status*, which is an indicator of her willingness to give her powerful support to one side in the conflict that continued to fester in the nursing world. And buried in the same speech, given to the Scottish branch of the RBNA in Edinburgh, she warns against 'opposition and misrepresentation we have hitherto had to encounter'. These were meaningful words, delivered at the time when pallid pronouncements by public figures were common and expected.

The RBNA, led for practical purposes, by its founder and Honorary Secretary, the redoubtable Mrs. Bedford Fenwick, was definitely *for* registration as a means of enhancing and guaranteeing the professional *status* of trained nurses. However, the incorporation of the RBNA by the Privy Council allowed it to maintain a *list* rather than a *register* of nurses.

In the end, the RBNA did not turn out to be the sole vehicle for the introduction of registration, which had to await many controversial years (and six attempts in the House of Commons) before the necessary Act was passed by the House on December 23, 1919.

The granting of the Charter to the RBNA can now be seen as significant in that 'it was the first occasion that a Royal Charter was granted to an association of professional women...'[137]. Typically, Princess Christian herself had no problems with being on the side of angels in battles for the advancement of women - in this case, the *battle of the nurses.* This was despite the warnings from no lesser a figure than Florence Nightingale herself (who was opposed to registration) that the Princess' involvement in such controversies might pose some danger to her prestige[138].

Princess Christian was very clear about the importance of registration. As early as 1895, she was addressing some typically forthright sentences to the general public. 'It is ..... confidently hoped' she wrote 'that the time is not far distant when all those who employ nurses ...... will decline to repose confidence in any nurses but those whose testimonials undergo the searching scrutiny of the Registration Board of the now incorporated Royal British Nurses' Association'.

She was also well briefed for the fight and was sensitive to political factors. For example, she pointed out that the 'honour of having first suggested and carried out the idea of employing trained nurses ..... is mainly ...... due to Mr. Rathbone, a philanthropic Member of Parliament'. The 'movement received powerful impulse when the Queen devoted the surplus of the sum ..... subscribed ..... on the occasion of her Jubilee, to the maintenance of nurses for the sick poor'. The Queen's Jubilee Nursing Institute which was funded by this surplus made sure that 'many of the District Nursing Associations have fulfilled the conditions of training required by the Queen's Jubilee Institute'[139]. Of course, she did not mention that her mother did not approve of women studying for *any* profession[140].

Princess Christian's stand in the matter of the professional status of nurses was particularly interesting in that she publicly supported something that was not altogether dissimilar from today's call for 'women's rights', and did so against the background of her mother's opposition to 'the movement for the greater emancipation of women' to which she was 'thoroughly and almost blindly antipathetic'.[141] In this as in many other respects the Princess does not appear to behave as the compliant and pliable - not to say dull - character that she is sometimes alleged to have been[142].

The Princess eventually lost her *personal* battle for the leadership of the nurses: when Alexandra, the Princess of Wales, became Queen on the accession of her husband to the throne as Edward VII, she directed her attention towards the Army Nursing Services and insisted on replacing Princess Christian as head of these services. This gave rise to considerable ill feeling, with the King caught in the middle between his sister and his wife[143].

Rank was all in situations like this, and the Princess had to resign in favour of the Queen. She did, however, retain her presidency of the Army Nursing Reserve which was initially thought to be an artefact created by society ladies, but which the Princess tried to run with her usual authority and efficacy. Her fundamental principle in situations like this was that 'she would never consent to be a mere figure head[144].

Typically for her, the Princess adopted a constructive stance when, at the age of 71, she publicly supported the proposed amalgamation of the Royal British Nurses' Association (of which she was the President) and the more recently formed (now Royal) College of Nursing. However, after protracted negotiations, the Council of RBNA eventually withdrew from the amalgamation process.

Thereafter, and especially after the Nurses' Registration Act of 1919 and the associated creation of the General Nursing Council, the RBNA declined in membership and influence, and the RCN eventually emerged as the totally dominant professional nursing body that it is today.

Princess Christian's interest in nursing extended to founding the Home for Nurses in Windsor, the Princess Christian District Nurses organisation and many other such enterprises. Her very consistent work in establishing nursing and hospital facilities for the poor, especially in Windsor, was based in part on her steadily increasing knowledge derived from close personal study of English, French and German hospitals. She was also involved in other nursing organisations. For example, she was president of the Isle of Wight,

Windsor and Great Western Railway branches of the Order St. John of Jerusalem[145]. She was very diligent in performing her duties and signed and presented many thousands of certificates of proficiency in nursing.

Needlework was among Helena's other major interests. Indeed *The School of Art Needlework* was founded in 1872 with Princess Christian as president. It acquired the prefix *Royal* in 1876 and the word *Art* was dropped from its title in 1922. The objective was - in Princess Helena's own words - 'first, to revive a beautiful Art which had been well-nigh lost; and secondly, through its revival, to provide employment for gentlewomen who were without the means of a suitable livelihood'. It was a way of preserving and developing the art of ornamental needlework and of passing the associated considerable skills to successive generations.

The Royal School was first located in Sloane Street in Central London but, with its increasing popularity, the premises became too small and the School was moved to Exhibition Road in London and then again to a specially built premises in the same road. The latter were opened on April 29, 1903 by the Prince of Wales (subsequently King George V) with much pomp and circumstance. The splendid Victorian building used to stand on the site now occupied by the ugly edifice that nowadays proclaims itself as the Imperial College of Science, Technology and Medicine. The original building. erected at great expense, was demolished in 1962. The School moved to 25 Prince's Gate and hence to its final destination, the Hampton Court Palace, where it still flourishes today.

The School was a costly enterprise to maintain, and in the several decades of her presidency, the Princess worked tirelessly and successfully to keep it on an even keel. Her managerial and business leadership, not to mention her concerns for the welfare of working women, emerge very clearly from her letters. They are free from what may now be called Victorian flannel and are very business-like and to the point:

'May I submit to you' - she wrote from Cumberland Lodge in 1895 in one of her appeals for funds - 'for your kind consideration this my appeal for assistance in raising £30,000 towards the work of erecting a building for the Royal School of Art Needlework at S. Kensington. The Royal Commissioners have of that I can raise within three years sufficient money to erect a building .... ' She even managed to squeeze £150 per annum from the Technical Education Board of the London County Council.

The activities of the School had a social side to them too. The Thursday Afternoon Tea parties held at the school were significant social occasions attended by splendidly attired society ladies anxious to be seen in the light reflected by royal personages such as H.R.H. Princess Christian (who was there more often than not) and other Royals. This generated considerable publicity that was helpful in raising funds. The Princess went to the length of acting as chief saleswoman at the Christmas Bazaar, and there were long queues waiting patiently to be served personally by the Princess.

This was not the only direct contact of the Princess with the public. For example, in February 1886, the Princess assisted at the Windsor Guildhall at one of the free dinners which she introduced for the benefit of the children and the unemployed of Windsor. She did so again several times during the following March. A total of over 3,000 meals were served to children and unemployed men during the severe winter of that year.

'She was a dear lady and like a mother to us' - was a typical comment[146]...... 'She was interested in many things and did an enormous amount of good that did not appear in the newspapers, and the poor of Windsor worshipped her'.

Laudanum

A unique glimpse of Helena's personality was recorded by the Royal physician, Sir James Reid[147].

Dr. Reid noted in his diary that Helena was suffering from severe hypochondria and, as a consequence, was a frequent user of opium and laudanum (tincture of opium, containing about 1% of morphine). Both the Queen and Prince Christian were aware of this and wanted Sir James to try to wean her off these drugs. It seems that he achieved a measure of success although he was not very sympathetic (at one point, he commented - in a flare of exasperation - that she was not a 'very satisfactory person to understand reason or logic').

In fact, laudanum was frequently and widely used as a general palliative by people who would not necessarily be classed as 'addicts'. For example, Charles Dickens used laudanum to steady his stomach and his nerves, and to help him sleep[148]. Florence Nightingale took opium on her return from Crimea to reduce stress and alleviate back pain, and Prime Minister W. E. Gladstone took laudanum in coffee before appearing before the House of Commons[149]. Even the Queen may have tried it.

Another physician (and dentist) who was a great friend of the Princess was a Dr. Wh. Fairbank w o attended her at Cumberland

Lodge and was for 37 years a Surgeon-in-Ordinary to the Christian's Household[150] (he died of apoplexy on the way to see the Princess at Cumberland Lodge in February 1880).

The question of Helena's ill health was emphasised by the Queen in her letters to her daughter Vicky. She believed that Helena's complaints about her poor health were encouraged by an indulgent husband. In March 1869, the Queen wrote[151] from Windsor Castle to Vicky that Lenchen 'was often complaining' and that 'she is so inclined to coddle herself (and Christian too) and to give way in everything that the great object of her doctors and nurse is to rouse her and make her think less of herself and of her confinement ….. '. In October 1873, she wrote to Vicky: '[Beatrice] is not touchy like several of her brothers and sisters are. That has increased with poor Lenchen (partly from poor health and partly from Christian's inordinate spoiling and the absence of all actual troubles and duties) to a degree that it makes it very difficult to live with her. ……..it grieves me ….. to see what poor health she has. She won't either do anything to get better and says she don't [sic] care if she is ill or well'. Clearly, the Queen didn't seem to appreciate Helena's hard work at St. Martin's Place and elsewhere.

Princess Helena's alleged hypochondria seemed to preoccupy the Queen, and it was certainly convenient to have someone relatively unexcitable like Prince Christian to blame.

On the other hand, there were also many well-documented episodes of poor health. In 1869 the Princess had to abandon a trip to Balmoral when she became indisposed at the railway station. In the autumn of 1870 she had severe difficulties with a swollen 'rheumatic knee' and, generally, problems with her joints[152].

In July 1871 she was[153] 'laid up with congestion of the lungs'[154]. The Princess' health problems at that time were said in the Court Circular to cause 'much anxiety to members of the Royal Family'. The cause was believed to be an infection of the lungs. The response of the medical men in attendance was to recommend a 'change of air'. Accordingly, the Prince and Princess departed for Ischl on the Continent almost at once. They left their children with their grandmother at Osborne and did not return to Windsor until the end of the following April.

In the winter of 1873, Helena had to spend the winter in the south of France on doctor's orders[155].

These were not untypical events. The Princess' letters often mention episodes of illness, especially rheumatism which was quite severe even in her twenties.

The Princess also had some problems with her eyes in the late 1880s for which she went to Wiesbaden (in 1888) to undergo a cure with a 'celebrated oculist' called Professor Hermann Pagenstecher (who had been a surgeon at the London Eye Hospital in 1872-1880 and was[156] 'one of the greatest occulists in Europe according to the Queen')[157].

She stayed in Wiesbaden with her two daughters for three months in a leased private villa. This enabled them to sample the life of ordinary German people, which was quite unlike the Royal surroundings they were normally used to.

Naturally, things got worse with the advance of time. In June 1914, when she was 68, she was prevented by severe sick headache and sudden faintness from reaching Windsor from London[158]. This was particularly disappointing to her because June 4, 1914 was declared 'Helena Day'. 70,000 roses were sold to the public on that special day, with proceeds going to local charities. It was requested that all houses be decorated with flowers and the town suitably adorned. A total of £452 was collected, of which Princess Christian received £363 for her charities. Everyone concerned received a personal letter of thanks from her.

Windsor had much to be grateful for to Helena[159]. For example, in 1879 the Order of St. John of Jerusalem established a network of centres in which men and women were instructed in first aid to the injured. Princess Helena founded one such Windsor centre and became its president. She attended the lectures and passed a number of examinations for which she was awarded the Medallion. Thereafter, the Princess presented Certificates and Medallions to candidates that were successful in these examinations.

Princess Helena presenting St. John's certificates and medallions in the 1890s

In 1894 she started the Princess Christian District Nurses and bought two houses to accommodate them in Windsor. In 1902 two further houses were acquired in Clarence Villas and eventually became the memorial to Prince Christian Victor. The Princess Christian Nursing Home[160] came into being in February 1904.

The Princess' medical problems persisted throughout her life and she must have found it useful to have Professor Pagenstacher stay with her at Cumberland Lodge on his visits to England (he looked after the Queen's eyes as well, especially during the last few years of her life). Whilst her mother was seriously worried for years about the implications of Helena's eye problems for her general state of health, Sir James Reid did not think much of Pagenstacher's alleged cure, and Pagenstacher himself later admitted to him that there was not much wrong with the Princess' eyes. Indeed he thought that her ophthalmological symptoms were largely due to the side effects of stimulants and narcotics.

He prescribed placebos and they seemed to work. But the unanswered question is: what was there in Helena's personality that gave rise to these signs of emotional instability, which appear to have been known directly to only three people: her mother, her husband and her doctor? She was unlucky in that none of them had the degree of real understanding that perhaps she really needed at a personal level. She gave conflicting outward impressions: great steadiness at some times and unusual touchiness at other times.

She suffered internally from deep rooted personal difficulties. Her mother saw the symptoms, but was too preoccupied with her own problems - and with the affairs of state - to be able to help her. The only way out was for Helena to keep busy, which is precisely the strategy she adopted.

Schomberg house mysteries

When not at Cumberland Lodge in Windsor Great Park, the Christians first resided in the Belgian Suite on the ground floor of Buckingham Palace in London and, later, in Schomberg House at 78 Pall Mall. This was the London address printed on the headed paper of the many surviving letters from the Princess. And it was at Schomberg House that Prince Christian died in 1917.

In her very interesting *Memories*, Helena's daughter, Princess Marie Louise, refers to 'that dear old London house of my parents and also of my sister and myself'.

She recalls that Professor Richardson, the President of the Royal Academy after World War II, told her that Schomberg house was originally occupied by the Duke of Schomberg in the time of William II and later by Thomas Gainsborough the painter (and also Richard Cosway the miniature painter). A traditional 'blue plaque' proclaims this fact on the building at Nos. 80-82 Pall Mall, *now* called Schomberg House.

A picture of Nos. 80-82 appears in *John O'London's London Stories*, published in about 1912. It is described there as 'the residence of the Princess Christian' and its association with Gainsborough and Cosway is recounted. The same picture appears in Princess Marie Louise's book.

The question therefore arises as to which house was the London residence of the Christians: 77-78 or 80-82?

The history of Nos. 77-78 is clear. In the early 1860s, the Marquis of Ailesbury converted the two houses into one and acquired a new lease for the combined property, to run for 49.5 years from April 1862 to October 1911. The lease was assigned in May 1895 to Evelyn Viscountess de Vesci and in March 1900 to the Commissioners of H.M. Works. A new lease was obtained by the Commissioners in January 1912.

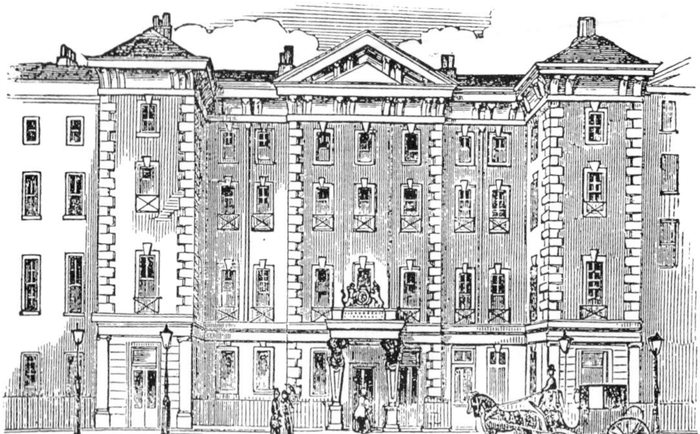

NOT the Schomberg House occupied by the Christians in Pall Mall

Searches through the *General Rate Books* of St. James' District No.1 for the first quarter of this century at the Westminster City Archive reveal that it was the combined Nos. 77-78 that were the home of the Christians. This is also clearly shown by voluminous correspondence relating to this property, which is held at the Public Records Office[161] in London (the relevant PRO file was 'closed' until 1983, presumably because of the Royal connection). Some files relating to No. 78 are said to have been 'destroyed' at the Crown Estate Agents.

The lease of Nos. 77-78 was left to Princess Christian by Queen Victoria when she died in 1901. The eventual instrument for this transfer was a Royal Warrant of August 9, 1902.

The property deal in which Nos. 77-78 were involved is interesting. It so happened that, in October 1898, The Royal Society - one of the foremost scientific institutions in the world (Sir Isaac Newton was a past President of the Society) - acquired the necessary funding from the Government for the *National Physical Laboratory*.

The first suggestion was that the laboratory should be built on an area of about 15 acres in the north east corner of the Old Deer Park in Richmond. However, there were strong local objections to this. The Richmond Town Council resolved[162] that this was a 'highly objectionable proposal' and the idea was dropped, which must have been one of the earliest victories for those fighting for the protection of the environment in England.

The next suggestion was that the new Laboratory should be located at Bushy House in Teddington, a small riverside town of about 14,000 inhabitants on the edge of London, which had remained empty for some years.

Prolonged negotiations between Government departments, the Queen's private secretary and The Royal Society, finally resulted in a formal offer from Windsor. The Queen's private secretary, Sir Arthur Bigge wrote in 1890 as follows: '..... Her Majesty by her Grace and Favour agrees to hand over to the Commissioners of Works the House and Grounds at Bushey [sic] ...... to be used by the Royal Society for the purpose of a Physical Laboratory. .... In consideration of Her Majesty's act .... the Government will place the de Vesci House in Pall Mall, rent free and in order for occupation, at the disposal of Her Majesty ..... as a Grace and Favour residence under the usual conditions as Her Majesty may think fit.' And Francis Moffat confirmed from the Treasury that that property would be handed over 'in good repair and fit for occupation free of rent'. He also confirmed that the Rates on the house would be paid by the Treasury[163].

The de Vesci House was the property at No. 78, which incorporated No. 77, and the lease upon it was purchased by the Commissioners of H.M. Works for £6,000 from Viscount de Vesci in 1900. And although it was called de Vesci House at the time, it was subsequently (in 1906) renamed Schomberg House.

The lease was transferred to Princess Christian, after the death of Queen Victoria, in the same year that the National Physical Laboratory was formally opened by the Prince and Princess of Wales and was destined to become one of the foremost scientific institutions in the world.

Following the death of King Edward VII, attempts were made by the Commissioners of Works to get the Christians to contribute to the cost of running Schomberg House. External and structural works were paid from Votes of Parliament, but internal works - it was suggested - 'should be defrayed by the Occupier'. To this the Comptroller of the Christian household, Major J. Evan B. Martin, replied that 'their Royal Highnesses were not even aware that there was a lease on the house with conditions attached. Their Royal Highnesses only admit to their liability to keep the interior in good repair.'

After Princess Christian died, the house was occupied by her daughters Helena Victoria (Thora) and Marie Louise (Louie)[164]. Again the Commissioners tried to reduce their outgoings by moving the two Princesses out of Schomberg House. The Princesses replied that the King assured them that they would not be disturbed for the rest of their lives[165]. And they stayed on.

The history of Nos. 77-78 thus clearly shows that the building *now* called Schomberg House (Nos. 80-82) is not the original house that was occupied by the Christians. The original Schomberg House was damaged by incendiary bombs during the war. A bomb at the end of St. James Street blew in the doors and made a mess of the interior.

Helena after the Devonshire House fancy dress ball

The house was returned to the Commissioners of H.M. Works in the late 1940s after the death of Marie Louise's sister. Marie Louise herself moved to a large top-floor flat at 10 Fitzmaurice Place at the bottom of Curson Street. The flat was given to her by George VI (it was originally prepared for the Royal Family in case Buckingham Palace was bombed). The Princess died in 1956, and despite having lived in 'modest circumstances', left about £130,000 in her will - a not inconsiderable sum in those days[166].

Because of the great interest of Princess Christian and her daughters in music, Schomberg House, with the excellent acoustics of its great *salon*, which stretched through the whole length of the house between Pall Mall and Marlborough House at the back, was at one time one of the leading private centres of musical life in London. Many world-famous singers and instrumentalists gave private recitals in Schomberg House.

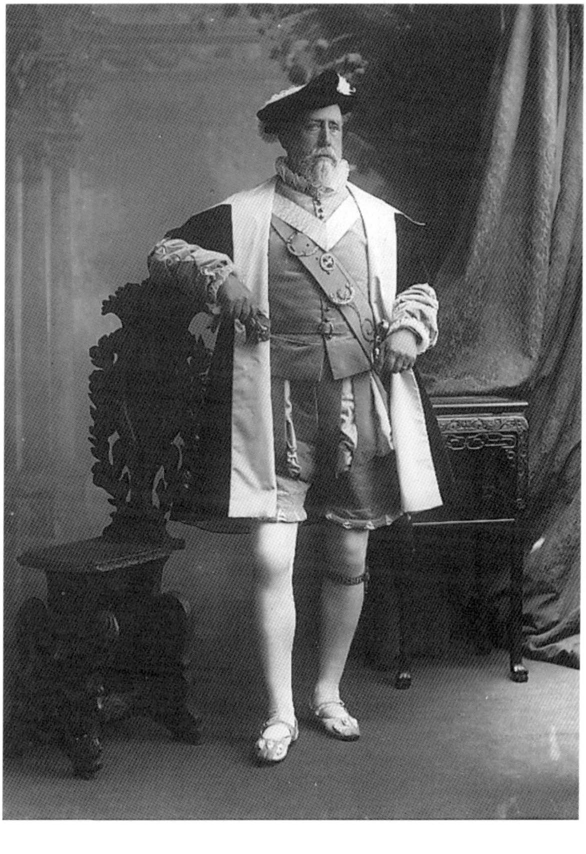

Prince Christian after the Devonshire Ball

The house was also conveniently located for all the events that engaged the interest of high society. For example, Schomberg House was not very far from Devonshire House in Piccadilly at which the famous Devonshire House Fancy Dress Ball was held on July 2 1897 as part of celebrations of the Diamond Jubilee of Queen Victoria. Naturally, The Prince and Princess Christian attended together with their daughter Helena Victoria. They were among some 700 other guests - the cream of Victorian society. The guest list ranged from the Prince of Wales (the future Edward VII) to A.J. Balfour (the future prime minister). A gaggle of famous photographers was on hand to record the individual guests of the Duchess of Devonshire who presided over the great ball. Prince Christian appeared as the Duke Adolphus of Schleswig-Holstein-Gottorp, and seems now no more ridiculous in his costume than some of the other figures[167].

Devonshire House was demolished in the 1920s when the rising cost of maintaining such properties in Central London resulted in the demolition of a number of these splendid houses and the impoverishment of London's architectural heritage, for which the owners of these properties must bear the major responsibility.

The residual question is: how was it that the wrong picture appeared in Marie Louise's *Memories* ? The answer may be that since the Princess died soon after the publication of her *Memories,* she may not have had the opportunity to check the illustrations introduced by the publishers' picture researcher into the final book.

The book appeared in 1956 and again in 1957, and was a great publishing success. It is often mentioned in the literature devoted to the period.

The picture of the house reproduced in Marie Louise's book was probably selected on the strength of the designation 'Schomberg House' which by then wrongly appeared above the doors of Nos. 80-82. Professor Richardson's anecdote about the house's history may also have been based on the misplaced name.

The entire Schomberg House mystery is neatly resolved by a typically fortright explanation given by Princess Helena herself in a letter despatched from Cumberland Lodge to Isabel Macdonald the secretary of the RBNA on October 9, 1917. In it the Princess writes: '..... we have given up the name Schomberg House and gone back to its original designation of 78 Pall Mall. The ignorant man in the street took into his head that Schomberg was a German name whilst it is *Dutch.* ..... So in order to be left in peace and avoid any more annoyances we have decided to resume 78 Pall Mall. It is sad people should be so foolish''[168]. When the contents of the London residence of the Christians were auctioned off in 1947 by order of Princesses Marie Louise and Helena Victoria, the auctioneer's catalogue[169] described the location as *Schomberg House, 78 Pall Mall,* SW1.

Unfortunately, the interiors of both *Schomberg Houses* were totally reconstructed in the 1950s and very little - if any - explicit physical evidence remains of those splendid days between the two world wars when the *soirées* were held in that splendid room at Nos. 77-78.

There were usually about fifty *invités* who were privileged enough to 'listen to world famous artists in an informal and intimate manner'[170]. Frieda Leider the Wagnerian soprano, Lauritz Melchior, Leon Goosens the oboist, Nicholas Orloff the violinist and many others sang or played to the comfortably seated guests of the Royal Princesses.

Prince and Princess Christian in ca. 1910

The present occupiers of the Pall Mall buildings - a shipping company and the Oxford and Cambridge Universities Club - are aware, in a general sort of way, of the royal associations of their buildings. But the local legend, related by an employee of one of them, seems to be that there are deep disused underground passages connecting the buildings to Buckingham Palace, which have not been looked at for several decades. Perhaps there is still more to be discovered about *both* Schomberg Houses.

Whilst the negotiations for Schomberg House were prolonged, but not particularly difficult, by 1911 a number of difficulties arose at Cumberland Lodge. The Lodge had to be modernised and the necessary work was so extensive that the family had to return to Frogmore House and did not move back until the spring of 1913[171]. Here, too, there was a legend about underground passages and secret links to the Castle. The Lodge was indeed connected to the principal Royal residence (in this case Windsor) by a tunnel big enough to allow a horseman to ride through it.

When the Prince died in 1917, by which time Princess Christian was in her early seventies, attempts were again made by the Commissioners and others to reduce the cost of running her households. It was suggested that the Lodge came with the largely honorary job of Ranger of the Park which the Prince held during his life. Now that he was gone, perhaps the Princess would contribute to certain expenses?

Her Comptroller, Captain Liddell, let this correspondence ramble on for a bit and then produced his trump card, namely, a letter from Queen Victoria, which simply said: 'I hereby grant the use of Cumberland Lodge in Windsor Park to my dearly beloved daughter Princess Helena Princess Christian of Schleswig Holstein for her life. (Signed) Victoria RI'. The note was dated July 14, 1888 and did not mention any running costs.

Since this was all very clear, Sir Frederick Ponsonby soon confirmed from Buckingham Palace that it was agreed with the King that there would be no 'variation of the conditions on which the house has hitherto been held'.

One would have thought that all these 'servants of the Crown' should have ascertained beforehand the true position with regard to both Schomberg House and Cumberland Lodge, so that the old lady would not have to be bothered by all this nonsense.

On the other hand, it is remarkable how Queen Victoria took prudent care to ensure that if anything untoward happened to the Prince, her daughter would be protected. Christian may have been given all kinds of honorary titles, but when it came to the crunch, the welfare of the Queen's daughter was of paramount importance to her mother. And so, in the end, all those years of Princess Helena's faithful service and companionship were at least partly repaid.

Cumberland Lodge passed into other hands[172] in 1923, but it is not clear what happened to its contents. And the contents of Schomberg House were disposed off by auction, conducted at Queensberry Hall in London by Messrs. Robinson and Foster on 24 -

25 March 1947 on the instructions of Helena's daughters[173]. The only item *The Times* considered worth mentioning was a 'pair of elbow chairs, upholstered in crimson silk damask, made for George III .... and later presented to Prince Christian of Schleswig-Holstein by the first Duke of Westminster.'

The final years

In October 1922, less than a year before her death, Princess Helena wrote[174] to her daughter Louise, enclosing £50 as her quarterly contribution. She explained that this was double the usual figure because Louie had extra expenses 'on account of your visits'. She also expressed her regret that she could not send more, but costs incurred at Cumberland Lodge were much higher than expected.

And then she told Louie, in the same letter, that she had received £7,000 to buy, alter and equip a house in Lancaster Gate in the Paddington area of London.

At first sight, this reference to Lancaster Gate is puzzling unless Helena was contemplating a move from Pall Mall, which, at her age at the time, was most unlikely.

A clue to the true answer to this puzzle is offered by Ordinance Survey maps for the early 1920s, which show an entity called *Helena Club* at No. 82 Lancaster Gate and the War Office Effects Branch at No. 81. It also turns out that a company called *Helena Residential Clubs Ltd.* was incorporated in 1921.

The Helena Club began operating at the combined Nos. 81 - 83 Lancaster Gate as soon as the monies received by the Princess could be applied to the reconstruction of the premises.

The aim was to provide facilities for women engaged in earning their livelihood and for all ex-service women. In the words of the incorporation document, the club was for women who at any time 'enrolled for full-time service in any corps under the direction of a British Government department'.

Helena Club continued at Lancaster Gate until the 1970s. The company that was formally responsible for running the club was wound up voluntarily in 1977. Some of its original directors were recognisable establishment figures associated with Service charities, but Helena herself was not (and could not) be among them. It is therefore likely that the original monies mentioned in Helena's letter to Princess Louise came from these charities. Indeed the winding-up statement dealing with the affairs of the company shows the transfer of monies to the Royal British Legion, Women's Royal Naval Service and the WRAC Association. The total transferred was the then huge sum of £287,469.

The remaining Helena Club members were offered the membership of another service women's club at 52 Sloane Street in Central London. A club known as the Sloane Club is now operating from these premises as a purely commercial enterprise (although surviving members of the original Helena Club still have certain membership privileges). A portrait of a distinguished lady hangs in the common room of the club. It looks remarkably like a portrait of Louie.

Once again, Helena took the initiative in setting up an institution offering constructive help to women. No doubt she had to pull a few strings at the War Office and elsewhere to acquire the necessary leases at favourable prices. As usual, she succeeded.

The Helena Club was the prototype for the club in Muriel Sparks' novel *Girls of Slender Means* in which it metamorphoses into the *May of Teck Club.*

In her autobiographical *Curriculum Vitae*, Muriel Sparks describes the club as 'absolutely charming'. It was 'from time to time' her London home in the 1940s. She refers to its founder as 'the worthy Princess Helena'.

The bedrooms occupied by the 'girls' were somewhat spartan, but the public rooms of the club were impressive, and the splendid greenery of the Kensington Gardens just across Bayswater Road were very enticing. It cost only one pound 12 shillings and sixpence per week to stay at the club just after the war. This included two meals a day, and an extra two shillings and sixpence was charged for a guest's dinner or lunch. Maids cleaned the rooms and made the beds.

The rules of the club were relatively rigorous, but the institution is remembered fondly buy those who took advantage of the facilities offered by it. The premises were eventually incorporated in a major hotel in which no traces remain of its immediate predecessor - the *Helena Club.*

This was not the only *Helena Club* in London. The premises of the RBNA at 194 Queen's Gate were in effect another. It offered accommodation to nurses until the 1970s when declining membership necessitated a move to a house in North London and whence, in the 1990s, to an office in the Duke of York's barracks in Chelsea, by which time the membership stood at 'a couple of hundred'.

The only other reminder of Helena in London is Helena Road in Ealing, where the Helena School once stood. The school has long gone and a 1960s block of flats called Helena Court has replaced it.

After Prince Christian died in 1917 at the age of 86, Helena lived relatively quietly for another six years at Schomberg House and at Cumberland Lodge. When she too died, on 9 June 9, 1923, at Schomberg House, the valedictory address given by the Home Secretary in the House of Commons was precise in its expression of public appreciation: '... the keynote of her character and her life was that of sympathy with human suffering. It was practical sympathy, not confined to the mere expression of sorrow.....' He may have added that she was one of the first to succeed in demonstrating that, in Britain, Royal remoteness, mystery and accessibility could coexist in a way that could not be readily understood elsewhere. She was the first people's princess.

She continued to be active right to the end. On 8 February, 1923 she had a letter published in *The Times*, appealing for support for the Princess Christian College in Manchester, which was established in 1901 to train children's nurses and has continued to operate ever since.

On 25 May, 1923, Helena's faithfull lady-in-waiting Emily Loch wrote[175] to Emily Diana Baird, a friend of the Princess since her teenage days:

> 'Princess Christian desires me to thank you very sincerely for your kind letter and good wishes for her birthday. HRH was so pleased to hear from you.
> I am sorry to say she has had a second attack of Influenza and has been very unwell. She is rather better, but very much pulled down. Today she will not be allowed to leave her room or see the many friends and relations who would like to come to her as usual on her birthday.'

This was the first time in over sixty years of correspondence, that Helena did not write personally to her old friend. Influenza was followed by heart attacks and the Princess died two weeks later.

It was a magnificently stage-managed scene outside St. George's Chapel in Windsor as the gun carriage bearing the body of the Princess drew up at the west door of the chapel. Men of the King's Royal Rifles Corps - the famous 60th Rifles in which the Princess' son Christian Victor served - lined the steps of Queen Victoria's Staircase. With the King leading the mourners, it was a visually and emotionally stunning occasion[176].

The Princess was buried just down the road from Windsor, near her first home, with her husband next to her, in the Royal cemetery - a simple but dignified place behind the Royal Mausoleum in the grounds of Frogmore House.

Years earlier, on 13 January, 1901, her mother had noted in her diary that she attended Divine Service and ' ....Rested again afterwards, then did some signing, and dictated to Lenchen'. This was the last entry in the famous diary, and her daughter's name was thus the last she mentioned. She died soon after. And now they were both gone.

There are few mementoes of the Christians in Frogmore House: the four years they spent there are commemorated by two engraved portraits and nine caned maplewood chairs with their initials upon them. But in Cumberland Lodge, a couple of miles away, there are numerous photographs, often inspected by the many students and others who nowadays attend residential week-ends at the house. They listen to talks and relax in the congenial atmosphere of the splendid country house.

The Victorian bric-a-brac that would now be considered as depressingly awful has mostly gone, but the interior of the house, now much simplified as compared with the Spencer-Warren photographs, is dignified and pleasant, with many images of the family that once lived there displayed in rooms and corridors. There are no direct descendants alive today.

The Royal home that once received famous politicians and artists has now become the house of people who come to listen, to talk and to enjoy the pleasures of what Helena's great friend Louisa Knightley once described as 'a pretty place in the grand old park'.

אמא אמרה שיש לי פרצוף יפה,
אז למה שלא כולם יראו אותו?

הדביקו את הפרצוף שלי במקום הכי מגניב שתמצאו
כמו רכב מיוחד או כל מיקום אקזוטי אחר, צלמו באינסטגרם ותייגו:

#MOSES_FACE

(או העלו את התמונה לאפליקציית Moses Face בפייסבוק שלי).

אחת לשבוע אכריז בעמוד הפייסבוק
על צלם התמונה המגניבה ביותר שזכה
בארוחה בשווי 150 ₪

אגב, מוזס ידידותי לסביבה, אז הימנעו מלהדביק אותו ברחבי העיר.

Appendix

Trained Nurses and Nursing in England

(An article written by Princess Christian and originally published in *Woman at Home* in 1895)

Among the many subjects which occupy the attention and enlist the sympathy of those who desire to devote their energies to helping others, there is perhaps none more important than that of the care of the sick and suffering. Rich and poor alike must, in the course of their lives, come face to face with sickness in some form or other, and feel the need of a helping hand.

The chord which Miss Nightingale struck when England's wounded sons were languishing in the East, vibrated throughout the land, and awoke that powerful and widespread impulse which has gradually revolutionised the nursing of the sick, and raised it to the rank of a profession. England will never forget that, at a time when the strongest prejudice existed against women taking an active part in public life and work, she it was who, with the help of a few devoted followers, laid down the lines of a new career for women, which has proved to be of national importance and for the benefit of humanity in general.

Although for long years Miss Nightingale has been unable to take any active part in the work which is so specially her own, she cannot fail to look with infinite satisfaction on the results of her labours, and to see on every hand members of her own sex fulfilling efficiently, and with universal approval, a mission which was formerly regarded as both unbecoming and unwomanly.

It is happily not as nurses alone, however, that women claim to take an active part in great work of utility. As it is a subject which must engage the thoughtful attention of women of all countries, a short sketch of what has bee done in England for the better care of sick persons may be of interest.

Speaking generally, nursing has become divided into three great branches - those who, under the nomination of the Queen's Jubilee nurses or District Nurses, visit the sick poor in their own homes; those who by special arrangement attend in private houses; those who devote themselves to the sick in hospitals.

The honour of having first suggested and carried out the idea of employing trained nurses, acting under organised supervision, to minister to the wants of the sick poor in their homes, is mainly, if not entirely, due to Mr. Rathbone, a philanthropic Member of the British Parliament. The movement received a powerful impulse when the Queen devoted the surplus of the sum which was subscribed by the women of the United Kingdom, as a proof of their devoted and affection, on the occasion of her Jubilee, to the maintenance of nurses for the sick poor.

The resulting organisation or institution is presided over and controlled by a specially appointed committee, and has its head-quarters in London, in the home of an old foundation known as St. Katherine's. It was instituted by Queen Catherine, and in those days was a hospital.

The Queen's Jubilee Nursing Institute has branches in Scotland and Ireland, both of which are doing excellent work. Many of the District Nursing Associations have fulfilled the conditions of training required by the Queen's Jubilee Institute, and have become affiliated to it.

The nurses who attend to patients among the well-to-do classes in their own houses differ widely as to training and efficiency. They all wear a professional dress, but the extent of their training varies from two or three months to as many years. Public opinion is, however, being gradually educated to expect some definite standard of efficiency, and happily the number of nurse-training institutions and employment agencies which insist on a high standard is gradually increasing.

The nurses employed in hospitals, and trained in the Institutions which are attached to many of them, vary, as has already been mentioned, both as to training and efficiency in a somewhat bewildering degree. But order and some approach to uniformity of standard are being gradually evolved out of the confusion which has hitherto been almost inevitable.

The Committee of the House of Lords, which has been appointed to enquire into the condition and management of the great London hospitals, has definitely pronounced that no nurse should be considered adequately trained and entitled to receive a certificate of efficiency in less than three years. Before that important judgement had been given the Royal British Nurses' Association, of which I have the happiness and privilege to be the President, decided to enforce the three years' standard on its members and on those who might desire to be inscribed on its list or register.

Within the present year the Lords of the Queen's Privy Council have decided that it is for the public good that the Association should be incorporated by Royal Charter, with special view to the maintenance, for the benefit of the public and medical profession, of its List of Trained Nurses.

It is therefore confidently hoped that the time is not far distant when all those who employ nurses, and especially members of the medical profession, will decline to repose confidence in any nurses but those whose testimonials have undergone the searching scrutiny of the Registration Board of the now incorporated Royal British Nurses' Association.

It must not be supposed that the functions of the Association are limited to those which have just been mentioned. It devotes much of its labour, and one-fifth of its income, to the relief of members; that is, nurses who either through illness, accident, or pecuniary losses, are in need of help.

Indirectly the Association exercises a great and always increasing influence. It has powerfully contributed to raise the standard of education and training in many schools of nursing, not alone in the United Kingdom, but also in the Colonies.

With what deep and warm interest we in England watch and note every step taken by our sisters of the great western continent in the spheres allotted by Providence to their distinctive gifts, it would be scarcely possible for me to express, but let us one and all find support and encouragement in the mutual assurance that the pursuit of great and noble ends is inspiring our hearts with generous emulation, and knitting them together in sympathy.

Acknowledgements

I wish to thank Her Majesty Queen Elizabeth II for graciously allowing me to reproduce photographs and to cite manuscripts held in the Royal Archives and elsewhere. I am greatly indebted to the following persons who generously responded to my pleas for help (but who bear no responsibility whatever for the text of this book):

At King's College London:
Professor Arthur Lucas
Professor R.E. Burge
Professor E.R. Pike FRS
Mr. D. Glass
Dr. Keith Powell
Miss Anna Morawska
Dr. David Green
Mr. David Metzger
At Cumberland Lodge, Windsor Great Park:
Dr. John Cook
Dr. G. Williams
At the Royal Archives in Windsor Castle:
Sir Robin Mackworth-Young
Mr. O. Everett
Lady S. de Bellaigue
Miss Frances Dimond
Thanks are also due to:
Mrs. Marlene Eilers Koenig
Mrs. Virginia Murray,
Miss A. Barrett, Imperial College London
Miss. H. M. Campbell, Royal British Nurses' Association
Miss S. McGann, Royal College of Nurses
Miss P. Methven, King's College London
Miss A. Kearns, British Red Cross Archives
Mr. Geoffrey Berger
Mr. John Hanson
Mr. Ian Shapiro

Sources

All relevant sources listed on the National Register of Archives as well as many of the documents in the author's own collection were consulted

[1]B. Disraeli,*Vivian Grey*, Cassell, 1968
[2]J. Richardson, *History Today* **27**, 350, 1977
[3]Roy Jenkins,*Gladstone*, Macmillan, 1995
[4]B. Connell, *Regina v Palmerston,* Evans, 1962, p. 339
[5]*Ibid.* p. 341.
[6]R. Blake, *Disraeli*, Oxford University Press, 1969
[7]*The Letters of Queen Victoria*, series I, II and III
[8]E. Longford, *Queen Victoria's Doctors*, in: M. Gilbert *A Century of Conflict,* H. Hamilton,1966
[9]*The Times*
[10]D. Bennett, *Queen Victoria's Children*, Gollancz, 1980, p. 89; H. Bolitho (ed.), *Prince Albert and his Brother*, 1933, p. 86; J. M. Packard, *Queen Victoria's Daughters*, St. Martin's Press, 1998; J. van der Kiste, *Queen Victoria's Children*, Sutton, 1990
[11]*The Letters of Queen Victoria*, series I, II and III
[12]J. Eagle, *Country Life*, September **8**, 615, 1977
[13]RA M21/100
[14]W. L. Arnstein, *The Historian,* **58**, 295, 1966
[15]RA M21/101
[16]R. Fulford, *Dearest Mamma,* Evans, 1968, p. 297
[17]O. Everett, letter dated November 3, 1998
[18]*Ibid.*
[19]The two letters cited here are in the posesion of Ruland's surviving family who have kindly supplied copies; the translation from German is by David Metzger.
[20]*The Letters of Queen Victoria*, series I, II and III
[21]R. Fulford, *Darling Child*, Evans, 1976
[22]J. Wake, *Princess Louise,* Collins, 1988, p. 130
[23]P. Crabites, *Victoria's Guardian Angel*, Routledge, 1937, p.163
[24]S. Dodgson Collingwood, *The Unknown Lewis Carroll*, Dover, 1961, p. 358
[25]J. Wake *ibid.*, p. 116; G. St. Aubyn, *Queen Victoria*, Sinclair-Stevenson, 1991, p.417
[26]Professor E. J. Burge, *private communication*
[27]B. A. Toole, *Ada, the Enchantress of Numbers,* Strawberry Press, 1992, p. 301
[28]*Fine Art Quarterly Review,* pp. 27-39
[29]*Visual Resources*, III, 167, 1986
[30]H. and A. Gernsheim, *Queen Victoria*, Longmans, 1959
[31]The British Library catalogue lists this edition and also a reprint by J. Murray
[32]Sir Robert Mackworth-Young, letter dated March 7, 1974

[33]1884; various subsequent editions
[34]*The Letters of Queen Victoria*, series I, II and III
[35]T. Martin, *Life of HRH Prince Consort*, vol. 2, p.175
[36]P. Crabites, *ibid.*; E. F. Benson, *Queen Victoria*, Barnes & Noble, 1992, pp. 189-195
[37]*The Times*, June 11, 1923
[38]J. Wake, *ibid.*, pp. 110-111
[39]Grey papers
[40]R. Fulford, *Dearest Mamma,* Evans, 1968, p.253
[41]*Ibid.*
[42] Grey papers
[43]*Ibid.*
[44]*Ibid.*
[45]*Ibid.*
[46]*Ibid.*
[47]Augusta Stanley, *Later Letters,* Cape, 1929, p. 157
[48]*The Letters of Queen Victoria*, series I, II and III
[49]R. Fulford, *Your Dear Letter*, Evans, 1971, p. 56
[50]Sir Frederick Ponsonby, *Recollections of Three Reigns,* Qartet Books, 1951; *Sidelight on Queen Victoria,* Macmillan, 1930
[51]R. Fulford, *Dearest Child* and *Dearest Mamma,* Evans, 1964 and 1968, resp.
[52]D. Duff, *Victoria Travels*,1970, p. 293
[53]A. H. Beavan. *Popular Royalty,* Sampson Low, Marston & Co., 1897
[54]J. Cartwright (ed.), *The Journals of Lady Knightley of Fawsley*, Murray, 1915
[55]Augusta Stanley, *Later Letters,* Cape, 1929, p. 52
[56]Knightley papers, Northhampton Archives
[57]Grey papers
[58]*The Gazette,* June 1866
[59]*Windsor Express*
[60]T. A. Macnaughten, *Windsor in Victorian Times,* publ. by the author, 1975, p. 62
[61]Princes Marie Louise, *My Memories of Six Reigns*, Evans, 1956
[62]Grey papers
[63]*Ibid.*
[64]H. Hudson,*Cumberland Lodge*, Phillimore, 1997
[65]J. Wake, *ibid.,* p.165
[66]See ref. 116
[67]The Earl of Bradford, Weston Park, Shropshire (copy kindly supplied by Ellen L. Hawman of *The Disraeli Project)*
[68]J. Cartwright (ed.), *The Journals of Lady Knightley of Fawsley*, Murray, 1915
[69]Marquis of Zetland, *The Letters of Disraeli to Lady Bradford and Lady Chesterfield,* Benn, 1929, p.37
[70]R. Fulford, *Darling Child,* Evans, 1976

[71]H. Hudson, *ibid.*
[72]Archive of Imperial College London
[73]D. Duff, *Hessian Tapestry,* Muller, 1967
[74]S. Lee, *Edward* VII, Macmillan, 1925, p. 475
[75]T. Herbert Warren, *Prince Christian Victor: The Story of a Young Soldier,* Murray, 1903
[76]N. E. Oxley, *A. Y. Nutt: In Service to Three Monarchs at Windsor,* 1996
[77] C. W. Cooper, *Town and Country,* p. 59
[78]*I bid.*
[79]M.A. Eilers, *Queen Victoria's Descendants*; Rosvall, 1997; B. C. Tompsett, Index to Royal Genealogical Data (http://www.dcs.hull.ac.uk/genealogy/royal/gedx47.html)
[80]E. Voules, *Free of All Malice,* privately published.
[81]Marlene Eilers Koenig confirms this in an e-mail dated 1998
[82]I am indebted to Mr. Guy Holborn, Librarian at Lincolns Inn, for this information.
[83]*Ibid.*
[84]After marriage, the newlyweds spent a month on a visit to Cumberland Lodge.
[85]H. Pacula, *An Uncommon Woman,* Weidenfeld & Nicolson, 1997, p. 361
[86]F. Ponsonby, *Letters of Empress Frederick,* Macmillan, 1928, p. 328.
[87]E. Voules, *ibid.*
[88]J.C.G. Rohl, *The Kaiser and His Court,* Weidenfeld & Nicolson, 1994, Chap. 8
[89]F. Esmarch, *First Aid to the Injured,* seven eds., Smith, Elder, 1882 -1907
[90]C. Grey (ed.), *The Early Years of His Royal Highness the Prince Consort,* 1868
[91]A. Taylor, *Laurence Oliphant,* Oxford University Press, 1982
[92]RA S31/69 and RA S31/69
[93]Augusta Stanley, *Later Letters,* Cape, 1919
[94]J. Cartwright (ed.), *The Journals of Lady Knightley of Fawsley,* Murray, 1915
[95]Letter dated 16 February 1884 in author's collection
[96]RA S31/69
[97]Marquis of Zetland, *ibid.*
[98]Marie Louise, *Memories of Six Reigns,* Evans 1956
[99]Lyton Strachey, *Queen Victoria*
[100]Marquis of Zetland, *ibid.,* pp. 36-37
[101]See ref. 116
[102]W. F. Moneypenny and G. E. Buckle, *The Life of Benjamin Disraeli, Earl of Beaconsfield*
[103]A. Maurois, *Disraeli,* 1928
[104]*Ibid.*
[105]F. Ponsonby, *Letters of Empress Frederick,* Macmillan, 1928, p.182
[106]*Alice - Grand Duchess of Hesse,* 1884 and other editions
[107] F. Ponsonby, *ibid.,* p. 328

[108]Private communication from Ruland's grand-daughter
[109]The letters cited in this chapter are in the author's collection
[110]*Leaves from the Journal* and *More Leaves from the Journal*, both published by Smith, Elder (1868 and 1884, respectively)
[111]I am indebted to Mrs. Virginia Murray for allowing me to see copies of some of the original documents in the archive of the publishers John Murray
[112]A copy of Martin's own *aide-memoir* about the agreement is in the author's possession as are copies of Bergsträsser's letters
[113]Marie Louise, *My Memories of Six Reigns*, Evans, 1956
[114]Marie Louise, *Letters from the Gold Coast,* 1926 and *A Choice of Carols,* 1925
[115]Augusta Stanley, *Letters,* Gordon Howe, 1927
[116]Hughenden Collection, Bodleian Library (brought to the author's attention by Ellen L. Hawman of *The Disraeli Project*, at Queen's University, Canada)
[117]Mends papers, NAM
[118]G. St. Aubyn, *Edward* VII, Collins, 1979, p.31
[119]*Lord Wantage, A Memoir by his Wife;* Emily Wood, *The Red Cross Story*; Beryl Oliver, *The British Red Cross in Action*; Wantage Papers; Westminster Archives.
[120]Westminster City Archives
[121]Wantage papers
[122]*Ibid.*
[123]*Ibid.*
[124]A. Roberts, *Salisbury,* Weidenfeld and Nicolson, 1999, p. 624
[125]T. Pakenham, *Boer War*, Weidenfeld & Nicolson, 1979
[126]J.C. de Villiers, Military History Journal (S.A.), **6,** No 3, 1984
[127]British Medical Journal, April 10, 1915, p. 653
[128]J. H. Plumridge, *Hospital ships and ambulance trains;* Report by the Central British Red Cross Committee, HMSO, 1902
[129]Letters in author's collection
[130]Warren, *ibid.;* T. Aronson, *Royal Ambassadors; The Times*
[131]*The Letters of Queen Victoria*, III, p.201
[132]*The Gentleman's Magazine,* 1797 and D. Clarke, *A Daisy in a Broom*, Julia London, 1991, p. 6
[133]J. Taylor, *Records of My Life*, 1832, p. 266
[134]A. H. Beavan, *ibid,* p. 188
[135]Princess Christian,*Woman at Home* 1885, p. 285 (see ***Appendix*)*I***
[136] RBNA Handbook, 1999
[137]S. McGann, *Battle of the Nurses,* Scutari, 1992
[138]A. Ramm, *Beloved and Darling Child,* Sutton, 1990, p. 156
[139]*Woman at Home*, 1895, p. 285
[140]A.M. Cooke, *Medical History* **26,** 308, 1982
[141]S.Lee, *ibid.*, p. 554

[142]N. Epton, *Victoria and her Daughters*, Weidenfeld & Nicolson,1971; L. Prole, *The Queen's Daughters*, Hale, 1973
[143]G. Battiscombe, *Queen Alexandra*, Constable, 1969, p.234
[144]A. Summers, *Angels and Citizens,* Routledge and Kegan Paul, 1988, p. 238
[145] Annual Reports of OSJJ
[146]C. W. Cooper, *ibid.*, 1935
[147]M. Reid, *Ask Sir James,* Hodder & Stouton, 1987
[148]P. Ackroyd, *Dickens,* 1990, pp. 772, 1019, 1052, 1071
[149]V. Berridge and G. Edwards, *Opium and the People*, 1987, pp. 59 and 65, resp.
[150]Windsor Express, November 3, 1917, p.6
[151]R. Fulford, *Your Dear Letter*, Evans, 1971, p.228
[152]Wantage papers
[153]J. Cartwright (ed.), *The Journals of Lady Knightley of Fawsley*, Murray, 1915
[154]*Ibid.*
[155]Marie Louise, *Memories,* p.20
[156]M. Lutyens (ed.), *Lady Lytton's Court Diary*, Hart-Davis, 1961, p.91
[157]S. Weintraub, *Queen Victoria,* Unwin Hyman, 1987, p. 560
[158]*Windsor Express,* June 6, 1914
[159]*Ibid.,* June 15, 1923, p. 5
[160]Marie Louise, *ibid.,* p. 124
[161] PRO CRES 35/2218; see also WORK 17/46
[162]E. Pyatt, *The National Physical Laboratory - A History*, 1983, pp. 22-25
[163]PRO WORK 17/46
[164]PRO CRES35/2218
[165]PRO CRES 35/2218
[166]E. Voules, *ibid.*; PRO CRES 35/2218
[167]*The Devonshire House Fancy Dress Ball*, published privately, 1899 (Kensington and Chelsea Library, London)
[168]RBNA Archive, item PC10
[169]The auctioneers were Robinson and Foster Ltd.; see note 144 below
[170]Marie Louise, *Memories,* p. 210
[171]H. Hudson, *ibid.*
[172]PRO CRES 35/2218
[173]I am indebted to the Hon. Mrs. J. Roberts for a copy of the auction catalogue
[174]Letter in author's collection
[175]D. Baird, *Victorian Days and a Royal Friendship*, Worcester, Littlebury, 1968
[176]*Illustrated London News*, June 1923

Index

Abbat (Albert), Prince 35
Albert, Schleswig-Holstein 64-65
Albert, Prince Consort 8, 10, 13-14, 17, 22, 24-26, 41
Alexandra, Princess (later Queen) 72, 122
Alfred, Prince 37, 39,
Alice, Princess, 12-13, 18-19, 30, 34-35, 44, 81, 84, 90
Arenberg, Valerie 65-67
Army Nursing Reserve 122
Arthur, Prince 59
Augusta, Empress William I 45
Baird, Diana 150
Baireuth, Margravine 29, 76-78
Balfour, A. J. 96, 140
Beaconsfield, Lord (see also Disraeli), 8, 72, 75, 78, 80
Beatrice, Princess 10, 30, 34, 46, 69, 128
Becker, E. 13, 17, 27-28
Bergstraässer, A. 79, 81-84
Bismarck 42, 44, 75, 90
Bismarck's Wars 90
Boer War 105
Botha, L. 24
Buckingham Palace, 3, 5, 9, 133, 138, 143-145
Bushy House 135
Carlisle House 112
Casanova, G. 111, 113-114
Chamberlain, J. 103
Charlotte, Queen 113-114
Chief Rabbi 9
Christian, Prince 1, 40, 43-54, 59, 60-63, 74, 79, 85, 88, 139-140, 143, 145,
Christian, Princess (see Helena)
Christian Victor, Prince 55, 62, 106
Chudleigh, E. 112
Clark, J. 9
Conroy, J. 7
Cooke, W. F. 21
Cornelys, Mrs. T. 115
Corrie (dog) 59
Cumberland Lodge 56-61, 70, 73, 144, 152
Devonshire House Ball 138, 140
Disraeli, Benjamin, 8-10, 48, 53, 56, 62, 65, 74-76, 78- 80, 89
District Nursing Association 122
Duckworth, R. 21, 35
Dunant, H. 92
Elimar, Prince 39
Fairbank, W. 127
Frederick, Duke 42, 44, 75
Frederick III of Prusia 34, 90
Frogmore House 34, 51, 54-55, 151
Furley, J. 94
Hesse-Darmstadt, Prince Louis 19, 90
Hughenden Church 8
Jameson Raid 101
Kent, Duchess 7
George III 66, 113, 145
George V 124
George VI 138
Gere, J. A. 28
Gladstone, W. E., 8, 48, 48, 72-73, 75, 101, 127
Goethe Museum 5, 28
Great Exhibition (1851) 61

Grey, C. 6, 36, 38-39, 52, 54, 71, 74
Hamilton, W. 11
Harold, Prince 56
Helena Club 146, 149
Helena Day 130
Helena (Princess) 1:
letters to Ruland 5, born 9, Lenchen 10, mother shot at 11, crush on Ruland 15, photos 16, 31, 57, 63, 138, 142, Queen's unkind references 31, 32, 46, 56, marriage plans 31, talent for drawing 88, Queen's companion 34, suitors 35-40, at Drawing Room 40, meets Christian 45, last birthday before marriage 46, wedding 48, Frogmore 51, finances 52-54, Christian Victor born 55, Albert born 55, Helena Victoria born 55, Marie Louise born, Harold born, stillborn son 56, Cumberland Lodge 56, staff 58, Christian Victor dies 62, Albert disappoints 64, illegitimate granddaughter 65-67, golden wedding 67, translates father's letters 71, Disraeli's friend 72-73, translates Wilhelmina's memoirs 76, translates Wilhelmina-Voltaire letters 78, introduction to Alice's letters 79, translates Esmarch 79, letters to Ruland 5, 80, Bergsträsser affair 80, Marie Louise's description 87, problem solver 88, good looking 88, at St. Martin's Place 90, cartoon 93, Red Cross 96, 99, public profile 98, trip to South Africa 100, 108, with Salisbury 102, hospital trains 105, at Christain Victor's grave 110, Princess Helena College 111-118, appearance later in life 118, accent 118, nursing 119, RBNA 119, Army Nursing Reserve 122, urses' registration 123, School of Art Needlework 124, serves meels 125-126, drug addiction 127-128, health 128-130, title to Schomberg Ho. 135-136, Helena Club 146
Helena Victoria (Thora), Princess 66, 69, 137, 140-141,
Horn, G. 77
King's College, London 21-23, 88
King's Royal Rifles 88, 150
Knightley, Louisa 47-48, 55, 88, 152
Koenig, Marlene Eilers 66
Kruger, P. 101-103
Laudanum 127
Lacock, C. 9
Lenchen (see Helena)
Leopold, King of Belgians 8, 31, 41,
Liddell, Alice 21
Lloyd-Lindsay, R. 91, 93
London Photographic Society 26
Lorne, Lord 19, 35
Louise, Princess, 12, 19, 39
Lovelace, Ada 24
Marie Louise, Princess 56, 64-69, 87, 118, 133, 137-138, 140-141, 146
Martin, Th. 73, 82
Melbourne, Lord, 8, 13
Mends, Col. R. H. 89
Milner, A. 102
Montague, J. 27
Murray,J. 62, 79, 84-89
National Physical Laboratory 135-136
Nightingale, F. 121, 127, 153-154
Nurses' Registration Act 119
Oliphant, L. 72
Osborne House 19, 37, 46, 55, 129
Pagenstrecher, H. 129, 132
Palmerston, Lord, 8, 41
Playfair, L. 61

Pompeati, Madame (see Cornelys) 115
Porphyria 66
Pouncey, P. 28
Princess Helena College 114, 116-117
Queen's Jubillee Nursing Institute 122
Royal Society 135-136
Raphael Collection, 15, 17, 25-29
Red Cross37, 92, 96-99, 105, 158
Reid, Sir James, 4, 9, 127, 131
Roberts, Lord 62, 106
Royal Archives, Windsor, 29
Royal British Nurses' Assoc. 119-123, 141, 147, 149, 156
Ruland, Carl, 1-15, 17-32
Ruland, C. F. 29, 80
Sahl, H. 15
St. John's Ambulance 71, 128, 130
St. Martin's Place 90
Salisbury, Lord 102
Schomberg House 2, 6, 134, 136-144, 149
Schulze, M. 20
Sell, C. 81
Sloane Club 124, 147
Smuts, J. 108
Spark, Muriel 148
Spencer-Warren, Mary 70-71, 151
Stanley, Lady Augusta, 13, 50, 54, 78, 88
Stockmar, C. 13, 20, 32-33, 38
Stockmar, E. 36, 38-39
Taylor, J. 115
Victoria (Vicky), Princess Royal, 10, 12, 19, 34-38, 41, 68, 72, 128
Victoria, Queen, 1-13, 17-20, 28, 33, 35, 40, 45, 48, 52, 56, 62, 66, 68, 72, 73, 74, 81, 87, 90, 117-118, 144, 151, 160
Voules, E. 65
Wagner, Valerie (see Arenberg)
Wellington, Duke13
Wheatstone, C. 21-25
William II, Kaiser 68-69
Williams, Sophie 113-115
Windsor Castle 6, 15, 17, 18, 25, 28, 39, 48, 51, 62, 107, 143
Würtzburg, E. 39